Silent No More

To Roxanne Rahbar
and family.
Thanks for all
of the support!

James Hope

Silent No More

Voices of Courage in American Schools

Edited by ReLeah Cossett Lent & Gloria Pipkin

HEINEMANN
Portsmouth, NH

Heinemann
A division of Reed Elsevier Inc.
361 Hanover Street
Portsmouth, NH 03801–3912
www.heinemann.com

Offices and agents throughout the world

Library of Congress Cataloging-in-Publication Data
Silent no more : voices of courage in American schools / edited by
    ReLeah Cossett Lent and Gloria Pipkin.
        p.   cm.
    Includes bibliographical references.
    ISBN 0-325-00471-4 (pbk. : alk. paper)
        1. Teachers—United States—Political activity—Case studies.   2. Courage—United
States—Case studies.   I. Lent, ReLeah Cossett.   II. Pipkin, Gloria.

LB2844.1.P6 S57   2003
371.14′1—dc21   2002151787

Editor: Lois Bridges
Production: Lynne Reed
Cover design: Joni Doherty
Cover illustration: Bert Lent
Typesetter: TechBooks, Inc.
Manufacturing: Steve Bernier

Printed in the United States of America on acid-free paper
07   06   05   04   03   DA   1   2   3   4   5

To my parents, Don and Page Cossett—RCL

To my parents, Don and Margaret Treadwell—GP

Contents

Introduction

When it is dark enough, you can see the stars.

—Charles A. Beard

*S*ince Socrates we've known the danger that extraordinary teachers can pose to the status quo, and the harms they suffer for their resistance to educational injustice. In the twentieth century, the brilliant Brazilian educator Paulo Freire was expelled from his university position, arrested, jailed by the military, and exiled from his country for his success in teaching peasants to read. But for the most part, in our own country, teachers are not viewed as transformative intellectuals. Instead, they are generally perceived—and often perceive themselves—as agents of the state, paid to do its bidding and transfer state-sanctioned facts and skills to their charges.

Every now and then a story comes along with a celluloid hero/heroine in the form of Meryl Streep, Michelle Pfeiffer, Edward James Olmos, or Richard Dreyfuss, a heartwarming tale about an educator who breaks the stereotype of the rather dowdy, soft-spoken academician. Audiences sit in mesmerized admiration as these teachers brilliantly and beautifully change the world for their star-struck students. Their stories, however, are not as rare as we might believe. For every face on the silver screen there are hundreds in the real world who resist the mandate to act in ways they know are not in the best interest of their students—and who face financial, professional, and social consequences as a result of their decisions.

The major stories collected here are those of contemporary heroes and heroines who have, in many cases, risked everything except their own integrity in stunning examples of civic courage.

But the pivotal question remains unanswered: Why is it necessary for those in the field of education to exhibit the type of courage usually reserved for threatening or combative occupations? The act of teaching requires a type of courage, as Parker Palmer points out in *The Courage to Teach* (1998). "The courage to teach is the courage to keep one's heart open in those very moments when the heart is asked to hold more than it is able so that teacher and students and subject can be woven into the fabric of community that learning, and living, require" (p. 11). But the voices emanating from these pages have gone far beyond keeping their hearts open. They have stood, sometimes alone, against an educational system tainted with political corruption, high-stakes testing, and fear. Their battles have left them unemployed, jailed, harassed, and isolated. Told separately, the stories create fragments of a frightening mosaic; told as one, the impressionistic tones blend together to form a bleak picture of the darker side of education in America.

Even the most breathtaking Hollywood special effects seem colorless compared to the story Steve Orel, adult education instructor, tells of 522 students involuntarily withdrawn from Birmingham, Alabama, city schools. Orel's persistence in uncovering the reason students were arriving at his classes with official withdrawal slips indicating "lack of interest" eventually led to his firing. Nevertheless, he continued to teach, without pay for a time, and created a haven for these students and others to continue their education, an opportunity withheld from them by their own city schools. What Orel discovered, even as he was maligned for initiating the quest, was the monster guarding the city gates: the low test scores of these students were threatening an already troubled school system. Throwing these students out of the mathematical mix would create higher averages and make the district appear to be improving in reading and math. The classist and racist overtones of this forced exodus, buried under a veneer of lies and denial, create the first wash of color in this powerful painting.

The forceful voices of two award-winning and popular teachers, Peggie Boring and Dr. Cissy Lacks, tell a different story, but its hues are the same. Alike in the magic they created for their students and similar in their pedagogical views, alike in the awards they accumulated throughout their distinguished careers, alike in their courage to defend the rights of their students and their own rights as teachers despite public humiliation and administrative retaliation, they epitomized ideal teachers. Creating an arena in which learning was a byproduct of authentic experiences and school a vehicle for the extracurricular activities that would come to define the lives of these student journalists, writers, and actors, they gave all they had. But once again, despite the outcry of parents and students, these talented teachers were relegated to defending themselves and their professional practices while those who had narrow conceptions of teaching and learning succeeded in driving them from the classroom.

Near Atlanta, another scene plays in full view of a national audience. Much like a small-town marshal in a Grade B Western, pistol on hip, eyes narrowed in distrust and suspicion, the local school police knock on the door of James Hope, fourth-grade teacher. Before it is all over, Hope and his wife are told they will be going to jail. Their crime? Releasing a few flawed test items that would never be used again, in an effort to help parents make better-informed decisions about the test that would be used as the only criterion to determine if their children would be promoted or retained. A few more splotches of color on the palette.

Are these merely pockets of despair? Places that don't accurately reflect the whole? Dr. Joanne Yatvin, commissioned by Congress to serve on the National Reading Panel, initially felt honored to be chosen for such an esteemed position. Soon, however, she began to feel uncomfortable not only with the process, but also with the hasty findings of the panel. Voicing her objections tentatively at first and then more assertively, she finally filed a minority report expressing her concerns that the panel's report was flawed, incomplete, and narrowly focused. Her report was virtually ignored, she was persona non grata in National Reading Panel presentations around the country, and, worse, the panel's hurried findings have now defined reading practices all over the United States. Despite the disfavor from the current national administration, Dr. Yatvin continues to speak out in behalf of children and against programs that ignore the complex variables of reading for each individual.

And what about the students of our classrooms? Their voices, as mere whispers, lack the power to oppose policymakers who hold their futures tightly in their fists. Even when students and their parents oppose high-stakes testing or demand basic intellectual freedoms, they are often powerless against the rumbling machines that oil and polish students to function smoothly in this global economy. It is left to teachers to serve as their advocates and stand with them as allies. Those we honor here have done just that.

In the first ten chapters, our readers will hear firsthand the powerful stories of these courageous teachers. The final chapter, "Portraits of Courage," includes shorter stories from around the country of those who have resisted high-stakes testing, one of the most serious threats facing education in the twenty-first century. For some of the educators (plus one community activist and a student) profiled in this section, the struggles haven't been as protracted nor the consequences as dire as those endured by the ten teachers featured in separate chapters, but we are inspired by and grateful for their examples. The courage of all those who refuse to "go gentle into that good night" shines brightly against a dark national tapestry.

Silent No More

1

Left Behind in Birmingham
522 Pushed-Out Students

STEVE OREL

STEVE OREL SPENT MOST OF HIS CAREER AS A BOILERMAKER AND CIVIL rights activist before he discovered the joys of working with adults and young adults "engaged in a second chance to continue their education." The workplace adult basic education program housed in a steel wire manufacturing plant on the eastern side of Birmingham seems the least likely place for the type of activism for which Orel has become nationally famous. But in a small cinder block building and the classroom trailer anchored in front of it, surrounded by a dirt parking lot pitted by the tires of those seeking a better life, a modest sign on the trailer leaves no doubt of the dream encased within these humble walls: World of Opportunity.

It was here that Orel unknowingly began a journey that would, indeed, give a second chance to many of the students who had been "pushed out" of the Birmingham City Schools. Orel's persistence in uncovering the real reason 522 Birmingham area high school students were involuntarily withdrawn from school cost him his job, but despite devastating setbacks he continues to insist that an educational world of opportunity should exist for every student, especially those whose lives are limited by circumstance, economic inequities, and an educational system in which they are offered no place.

*O*n a sunny March afternoon, sixteen-year-old Renae enrolled in the Birmingham City Schools adult education program where I had been teaching for four years. She reached into her purse and pulled out a folded piece of paper that I recognized as a form from the high school she had been attending. It was familiar to me because I had seen similar ones within the past week. Like the others, it said, "Withdrawal. Reason: Lack of Interest."

In all, I met fifteen withdrawn students, and some of their parents, from three area high schools. I began to question why three separate high schools were using the same form and the exact same language, "Lack of interest," to remove students from school. Other adult education teachers felt my questions were legitimate.

Some other common characteristics began to emerge. All of the pushed-out students I came in contact with were African American teenagers. These young people were officially ninth, tenth, eleventh, and twelfth graders, yet many of them were functioning at fifth-, fourth-, and even third-grade academic levels, as measured by the TABE (Tests of Adult Basic Education).

None of the students I met had voluntarily withdrawn. In fact, some had actually returned to the school with their parents or guardians and asked to be readmitted, but their requests were denied. Parents had not been included in the withdrawal meetings, and some parents did not even know their children had been withdrawn.

As I soon learned, these young people had not had a reasonable, nonthreatening, face-to-face dialogue with an adult in authority in a long time. I asked a lot of questions and listened carefully to their descriptions of how they came to be pushed out of school.

One by one, the students told chillingly similar stories. One fellow (real names of Birmingham City School students are not used in this narrative), Lindsay, explained, "I showed up for class and my teacher told me that my name was on a list, and he sent me down to the office. When I got there I saw my name was on a list, and they told me that I had to be withdrawn."

Bradley provided more details: "About two to three months ago, there was a school assembly. The principal spoke to us and said that he didn't want any students to interfere with the SAT scores. He said that the SAT scores were already low, and that the state was going to take over. He said that he would try to get out the students, out of the school, who he thought would bring the test score down. He also gave us this same message over the intercom a couple of times after that. On the last day that I went to school, I was told to report to the principal's office because my name was not on the roster. I was given a withdrawal slip which said, 'Lack of interest.' I did miss a lot of school days. I had family problems. I had allergies." Within two weeks of being withdrawn for "lack of interest," Bradley enrolled in a pre-apprenticeship construction training program *and* an adult basic education GED preparation class just a couple of miles from the school he was expelled from.

Renae's mother told me that she tried to get her daughter back in school but was informed that her daughter's scores were low and she wouldn't pass anyway. The mother insisted that she still wanted her daughter to remain in school so she wouldn't fall even further behind, but school officials refused to readmit her.

Lavonne told me she was put out on February 11. She remembered the precise date because it was her sixteenth birthday. Another youngster, Russet, told me he was pushed out of school on April 14.

"But, how do you know it was April 14?" I asked.

"Because I turned sixteen the next day, which was a Saturday," Russet told me. Now alarms were going off in my head. I heard that some students had seen a list with birthdays on it.

Most of the students readily admitted they had missed a lot of school. Pregnancy and medical complications kept some of the young women from attending regularly. One student, Autumn, who had a miscarriage, learned that she was withdrawn when she returned to school. Julie's baby died a couple of weeks after birth, but she received no grief counseling when she went back to school. Instead, she was withdrawn for "lack of interest."

Ladarius described how his older brother moved back home, terminally ill with cancer. When his brother became bedridden, Ladarius stayed home from school to care for him while his mother and sister worked. Within a couple of weeks, Ladarius' brother passed away in bed at home. A week after the funeral, Ladarius returned to school, only to learn that he was withdrawn for "lack of interest." I've spoken with his mother, who verified this tragic story.

Other students told me that they missed school because they were sick. Some had doctors' notes. Some students told me they were afraid to come to school because of gang activity. Others told me they didn't attend much because they didn't understand the instruction. Several students told me their teachers berated them, "You're not gonna amount to anything. You're gonna end up on drugs and end up in prison." They told me they just felt that they didn't belong there in school.

When I told one of my supervisors about the stories the students shared with me, she said, "You know these students lie." I responded, "But some of their parents have told me the same story." She quipped back, "You know that parents lie, too, to protect their children." I was dumbfounded at how jaded my supervisor had become.

Another event distressed me. The first pushed-out students I met presented withdrawal forms that were filled out by hand. Within a couple of weeks, students brought me *computerized* withdrawal forms. It was as though the miner's canary stopped chirping. I concluded that the number of withdrawn students must have been increasing if they resorted to computers to speed up the pushout process.

At first when I asked my supervisor the meaning of these withdrawals, she told me not to worry about it because it "enhanced adult education enrollment." Other supervisors and instructors were more candid. They explained that the students were withdrawn to remove low-achieving (i.e., low-scoring) students in order to raise Stanford Achievement Test, 9th Edition (SAT-9), scores. I also learned that six local high schools were placed on academic alert status by the State Department of Education. Low SAT-9 scores would mean some school takeovers by the state, and the local board of education was apparently willing to do *anything* to prevent that. Some principals had been transferred the year before, when SAT-9 scores did not get their schools off academic alert. What I didn't know at the time was that the superintendent's bonus hinged upon raising achievement test scores.

But why push students out *en masse* now, at this time of the year? Why didn't they push them out before, I wondered. I learned that the school administrators set their calendar for these withdrawals based upon state funding regulations. I was told that all students who are on the rolls on the fortieth day of the second semester (usually around February fifteenth) will be included for per-student funding through the rest of the year whether they actually attend school or not. So, on that fortieth day, those students in attendance helped ensure that their schools received their per-capita monies, but once that day had passed, on the forty-first day, these same students became an achievement test score liability. They used these kids to get funding, and then they discarded them like waste to get bonuses.

Since my supervisors were not interested in discussing this matter or helping to stop this practice, I raised it with Virginia Volker, one of the two student advocate members who was usually outvoted on the five-member board of education of Birmingham City Schools. She told me she had already heard similar reports from other parts of the city and that she was very concerned. When she inquired about the withdrawal situation at board meetings, she couldn't get straightforward answers. At one meeting, she asked, "How many students were expelled from Woodlawn last month?"

The superintendent offered her a terse one-sentence response: "No students were expelled in the previous month." That's because the operative word was "withdrawn," not "expelled."

Due to Ms. Volker's persistent inquiries, the withdrawal situation began to get some minimal coverage in the local newspapers and on TV. At first, board officials denied that students were being pushed out of school. The superintendent and high school deputy superintendent insisted there had been no mass withdrawals. They said that they had looked into the situation and there was no merit to Volker's allegations. However, within a few days, they conceded that 115 students had been withdrawn from Woodlawn High School alone. Convinced that the board would not rectify this injustice, I filed a complaint with the State Department of Education.

When I learned about these withdrawals in early March, I began working on a term paper for a graduate course at UAB (University of Alabama at Birmingham) School of Education. The paper challenged the significance and misuse of standardized tests. In it, I documented the withdrawals and included statements from some of our students, though their identities remained confidential.

Meanwhile, the board sank to an unconscionable level and began making a series of public statements demonizing the withdrawn students. They said these were "bad kids." They described them in such terms as "rapists, arsonists, thugs, hooligans, and gang-bangers," and claimed these students were "causing chaos in the schools" and "disrupting the learning process." With one broad stroke, they painted all of the pushed-out kids as criminal elements. They challenged critics to "walk a mile in our shoes. Try spending a week in class with these students and then you will understand."

Since I *had* walked in their shoes—by this time I had spent several months in class working with fifteen pushed-out students—I accepted this challenge. I told my boss that I felt compelled to speak out in defense of the kids I worked with and to refute these slanders. She told me to "speak from your heart," so I wrote a statement to a reporter (to ensure that I would not be misquoted) at the *Birmingham Post-Herald*. A news article in mid-June quoted my remarks.

"There hasn't been any horseplay, let alone a fight," I wrote to the newspaper. "There hasn't been any disruption or a lack of respect for the other students, our staff, or our volunteer tutors." Once enrolled, the students tried their best to complete their assignments. They applied for library cards and began taking books home to read. Those over eighteen registered to vote. They engaged in dialogue journal-writing assignments and began to reflect on their schooling, lives, careers, ambitions, and insecurities. One student designed a website.

I requested and received permission to keep our program open during summer (without pay), because I was convinced that our students did not "lack interest." If these students were willing to sacrifice first their spring break and now their summer to continue their education, then I wanted to be right there with them. When the students kept attending voluntarily, I was sure we were right.

Just before the article appeared, the newspaper reporter informed me that the school board had a copy of my term paper. I was astonished that my term paper had found its way into the hands of my employer, but I naively thought, "Good. Now the pushouts will stop and we will get these students back in school." I could not have been further off base.

After the newspaper article appeared, several other parents contacted me and described painful scenarios. When their children came home with withdrawal slips, the parents accused them of doing something wrong, somehow deserving being put out of school. Parents became angry with their children. Children felt that they had failed their parents and grandparents. These withdrawals caused many family arguments, tears, and much turmoil.

Determining the Truth, or Damage Control?

On June 27, my immediate supervisor instructed me to report to the deputy superintendent's office. When I arrived, Peggy Sparks, the director of community and adult education, was already there. While we were waiting for the deputy superintendent, Sparks told me that "speaking to the press is a no-no."

When Dr. Abbe Boring, the deputy superintendent, finally arrived, she explained that the superintendent, Dr. Johnny Brown, had instructed her to ask me two questions.

For a fleeting moment, a feeling of relief overcame me. The first question would no doubt be about the truth of my allegations that low-achieving students were pushed out of school to raise standardized test scores. The second question would be that if my allegations had merit, what could we do to retrieve these students, get them back into the educational fold, and correct this tragedy. But I was dead wrong.

First, the superintendent wanted to know who authorized me to write a research paper for my class at UAB.

Second, the superintendent wanted to know whether I had permission to make public statements to the press.

The deputy superintendent, on a mission of damage control, was only interested in discussing protocol, not the substance of the charges. At this meeting, the newspaper reporter's earlier warning was confirmed. Without my permission, my term paper was turned over to the board superintendent. I would later learn, in depositions, that the term paper was faxed to the superintendent on June 14, 2000, straight from the president's office at the university.

My speculation is that, in what they considered a preemptive strike, the board turned my term paper over to the newspapers, with a written refutation of the contents. Their refutation, dated June 15, 2000, titled "Recent Issues of Concern," read, "This week a graduate level term paper was provided to the school district which includes information similar to comments recently made by Board Member Virginia Volker. The term paper was reported to have been written by a Birmingham Adult Education Program employee and student at UAB. The research was not authorized by the School District."

On July 3, Wanda Minor, coordinator of the adult education program, asked me for a copy of my term paper from UAB. I told her that I didn't want to distribute it any further until we could resolve some concerns that the deputy superintendent raised regarding the content of the paper. When I told her that she could get a copy from my attorney, whom she knew, she became furious. "That's it! Your program is closed, effective today!" I told her that in March and April, the students were pushed out of school, and now, in July, she would be locking the door on our program, adding more injury. I pleaded with her not to take her anger toward me out on our students. I also said that I didn't see how she could stop me from teaching since I was there voluntarily, without pay, during the summer anyway. She was adamant that the program would be closed down immediately.

Devastated, all I could see in my mind were the inquisitive expressions on our students' faces as we studied together to pass the GED. Then I imagined their looks of disappointment if they heard we were shut down. How could I even muster the strength to break this news to our students? I kept the program open while I appealed Minor's decision to her boss, Ms. Sparks. The appeal meeting also abruptly ended when I did not produce my term paper upon request.

I was tormented about what to do. I could not stand the thought of students arriving by bus, or being dropped off, only to find the doors locked, with no explanation. My supervisor advised me that if I went back *in* the school and reopened it, that would be insubordination. I faxed the deputy superintendent and asked for immediate advice since I knew students would show up for class, and I felt they were owed an explanation. The deputy superintendent would not take my calls. So I decided that it would be OK to stay *outside* of the school, as I would still be following the directives not to go *in* or to open up the building. Beginning July 10, I went to our school site for three days in a row, and waited during class hours so that I could talk with the students about why the doors were locked. I gave each student a letter of encouragement, individually urging all of them to continue their studies and return when we were scheduled to reopen in the summer.

When the students arrived to find locked doors, some of them began to cry. Mrs. Ball, who regularly dropped her daughter off, was in tears. The same newspaper reporter who published my earlier statement in defense of the students was on hand to talk with students and parents, but she never printed one single word of this. Nearly two years later, I learned why she was silent and kept the pushouts and this closure a secret. I read in her own newspaper column of March 2, 2002, her words, "I've known [the superintendent] almost as long as he's been in Birmingham, and I happen to like him." She wrote, "He put teachers on notice that standardized test scores mattered."

Director Sparks assured me that all of the students would be referred to other programs, but I have yet to find the first student who was contacted and offered an alternative place to continue his or her GED studies.

About a week later, I submitted a proposal to the superintendent and the entire school board. On July 25, 2000, I made a presentation to the board that centered on a massive volunteer literacy project to work one-on-one with the withdrawn students.

After my allotted three-minute presentation, board member Virginia Volker asked the superintendent to confirm the number of students pushed out. Just how many students do you think were "withdrawn for lack of interest" prior to the administration of the SAT-9 tests?

The superintendent confirmed that there were 522 students withdrawn for lack of interest! The school administrators pushed out 5.6 percent of the entire high school student body. TV news crews and newspaper reporters were on hand, and I was relieved that finally the truth would come out. But the fact that 522 students had been administratively withdrawn was not even mentioned in any of the media's coverage.

How did the board respond to my proposal to retrieve these students? They fired me the next day, July 26, 2000.

I am not aware of any actions the board took to retrieve the withdrawn students. These kids were dispersed to the wind and the streets, with no direction and no supervision. Timothy Harrison, a pushed-out student from Woodlawn High School, was gunned down on June 21, two blocks from our school. His cousin, Berta, one of our students, poured her heart out in a loving tribute to him that she composed at our program. She wrote, "Timothy was a special child who needed someone to take time out for him, one-on-one. I know in high school you can't do that. But I feel like they could have done something besides giving up on him. Tim really wanted his education because if he didn't he wouldn't have gone the first day." Now, there were only 521 students to retrieve.

From the outset, administrators within the academic and teaching community warned me that my job would not survive if my allegations became public. Despite the fact that this career was one that I loved, there seemed no choice but to speak the truth, stand beside the students I worked with, and try to put an end to this standardized test–driven madness.

An extraordinary chain of events took place after I was fired. I was in contact with the National Center for Fair & Open Testing (known as FairTest) and shared events as they unfolded with their Assessment Reform Network (ARN) email list. ARN activists sent dozens of emails to the superintendent and board members, urging them to reinstate the pushed-out students and to rehire me. Volunteer tutors who worked with our program also wrote letters of support. My biggest inspiration came from some of the students who wrote letters in my behalf. Josie, an especially talented and mischievous youngster, wrote about the pains of being withdrawn, saying that our program was different and that she felt included there. She said that her instructor "makes ways out of no way." The administrators just couldn't "get it," but Josie did.

When the school system fired me, they failed to calculate the support our program enjoyed in the community. For the previous year, we had been sharing our facility with World of Construction, a job readiness program established by Brother Charles Todel of the Salesian Ministries, an order of the Catholic Church. Brother Charles was also the executive director of BAC (Be an Apostle of Christ) Foundation. When Brother Charles learned that I had been fired, he warmly embraced me and asked me to come work on his project, the World of Construction. The Salesians' mission is to work with poor and abandoned youth, and these 522 students were certainly poor and abandoned.

Brother Charles and I were truly an odd couple. He, an eighty-year-young Salesian brother and devout Catholic . . . I, a nearly fifty-year-old humanist Jewish fellow. He is steeped in the New Testament and the teachings of the Salesian patron saint, John Bosco. I am an eclectic scientific-materialist, standing on the shoulders of DuBois, Freire, Angelou, Twain, Tubman, Fritchman, my mother, and countless earthly others. Brother Charles practices the Salesian "preventative method" with youth, while I engage in Tikkun Olam (Hebrew for "to repair the world"). We were a match made on earth. We set aside theological and philosophical differences about the afterlife, and concentrated on life in our community: the suffering, pain, sorrow, joy, dreams, and ambition in the here and now. We are kindred spirits when it comes to offering encouragement to poor and working-class youth. We both wanted to help our youth find that untapped reservoir of talent, creativity, uniqueness, inquisitiveness, and potential that all human beings possess.

I worked for no pay from early June through mid-August to try and reopen the program. We expanded the World of Construction, which offered career exploration in carpentry, electricity, drafting, and masonry, to include GED and adult education, literacy, and English as a Second Language. We also added computers and AutoCAD (computer aided drafting). We renamed our new project BAC World of Opportunity, affectionately known as the WOO. In August, I was hired by the BAC Foundation, where I received eighteen hours' worth of pay per week for sixty-plus hours' work. I was going broke, but I wore a warm smile on my face.

Then we were joined by the third member of our trio, Carmen McCain, an amazingly talented registered nurse and civil rights advocate, who is also the founder and president of Mothers Against Violence. Carmen's son, Bonkey, was killed in a drive-by shooting on October 30, 1992, and she has been a leader in peace-building and antiviolence intervention ever since. Carmen's expertise and dedication allowed us to add health care and nursing training to our curriculum.

This unusual set of circumstances afforded me an opportunity to continue working with many of my same students; however, new troubles were brewing.

When Birmingham City Schools learned that I had been hired by another agency at the same location, they pulled out of the partnership completely. Ten days before we were scheduled to reopen, they pulled up with a truck, unannounced, and began taking boxes and boxes of textbooks and testing materials with them.

Despite this setback, the World of Opportunity opened its doors on September 5, 2000.

The owner of the manufacturing plant agreed that we could still use their building if I could keep the program going. I notified the FairTest Assessment Reform Network email list about what had happened to our books, and Susan Ohanian (Vermont) and Gloria Pipkin (Florida) organized a book drive appeal. The response was overwhelming. We have received more than five thousand books, which came pouring in from all across the country. More than a thousand books came from Charlie MacKay of Fogelsberg, Pennsylvania, "in memory of his beloved wife, Virginia McCormick, a lifelong educator."

The World of Opportunity has been open for nearly two years and remains a work in progress. More than 950 people have enrolled in our program. Our actual average daily attendance is twenty-five to thirty, and at least one hundred people are active in the program each month. We have now had contact with more than a hundred students who have been pushed out of their former high schools. They see the World of Opportunity as a second chance to continue their education and complete their dreams deferred. As much as possible, we are matching instructors and tutors to work one-on-one with our students in literacy, GED preparation, and career skills.

Just recently, we learned that Yolanda, a seventeen-year-old single mother, sailed over her GED exam. She is our seventh student to pass the exam. We are lining up an appointment for her to interview for a work-study program at a local college.

Demarquies, a twenty-three-year-old father, also catapulted over the GED threshold and became our eighth student to pass. LaTorria and D'Andrea became our first students to take and pass the new GED-2002 exam, and they did so "with flying colors," according to the testing center examiner. LaTorria has been accepted with a partial scholarship to the University of Alabama at Birmingham's Honors Program.

Although I am not a fan of the standardized GED test, we have no choice but to prepare for it because not having the GED is a legal obstacle to obtaining a driver's license and to many entry-level employment positions.

In August 2001, Brother Charles was dispatched by Salesian Ministries to establish a World of Opportunity program in Chicago, and I assumed the role of coordinator of our Birmingham program.

Our staff and volunteers are of all different beliefs, nonbeliefs, and persuasions. We are very ecumenical and we promote tolerance, unity, equality, restorative justice, and peace-building. In our curriculum, classroom discussions, and one-on-one counseling we confront problems our students face in their daily lives, such as racism, gang activity, peer pressure, and domestic violence, especially assaults against women. No subject is taboo or "off limits" if it is on the minds of our students.

Besides the academic and vocational components of the WOO, we actively work with our students to resolve issues such as hunger and poverty. The Salesians, with support from BAC, operate a food pantry directly across the street from the WOO, and we keep as much food as we can afford available at the WOO. Lately, our menu consists of instant microwaveable noodle soup, peanut butter crackers, and canned soda pop. We partner with other social service agencies to locate transitional shelters for our homeless students, or to find funds to avoid utility disconnections. We also have a small pool of volunteer lawyers who assist our students with their legal problems.

In nearly two years of operation, we have not witnessed within our program a single one of the problems the board accused these students of. Not a single argument. Not even a cuss fight.

Despite our optimism, all is not well at the WOO. More than seven hundred of the eight hundred students who signed up have not completed their goals. We have had tragic setbacks as well. We buried Mandrell, a twenty-two-year-old student who was studying for his GED. The streets devoured him.

As we identify and address academic and vocational goals, we also focus on immediate human needs. Our students come to school hungry. They come bruised physically from violence at home or in the community. They come with battered souls and sprits, with low self-esteem and a lack of confidence. Some face evictions, layoffs, and economic desperation. These young people show up at the WOO seeking a chance to make themselves a future, but it's hard for them to see very far ahead. They write essays that say, "*If* I turn eighteen, I want to be ..." rather than "*When* I turn eighteen, I want to be...." Many of their dialogue journal entries about happiness and joy are connected to grief and sorrow: "The burglar did not hurt me. That was my happiest moment."

Truth-telling has consequences that also affect my family. My journey has placed real hardships on my wife, Glenda Jo, and our son, Justin, but they have supported our students and me through this ordeal. Getting fired decimates your finances, ruins your credit, and puts stress on your family. It is a depressing feeling to receive your walking papers. Depression leads to fatigue, which leads to exhaustion. It's hard to get through a firing unless you are able to hold your head up, look forward, and keep pursuing your dreams and convictions. There's nothing politically romantic about being fired.

I never intended to work outside of the public school system, but after I was fired and sent into exile, this became the only way to continue working with and teaching these students. I filed a lawsuit to get my job back and someday I hope to return to the public school system, teaching at what is now the World of Opportunity, where I started. The suit alleges that I was fired for exercising my First Amendment rights when I made inquiries and spoke publicly about the students who were pushed out of school to raise test scores. The first oral arguments were heard April 9, 2002. The board of education has filed what appears to be a flimsy motion for summary judgment.

Although I am the plaintiff, the board has high-powered corporate lawyers who have all of the resources and power at their disposal to effectively turn me into the defendant. They have asked me questions about my wife, my marriage, and my son. They served subpoenas on my last three employers, and they sent their legal staff to the boiler shop where I worked for eighteen years, to rummage through and copy hundreds of payroll records and time sheets.

My privacy has been violated. I have been slandered in depositions, in the community, and in letters sent out of state. It has been very difficult to build the World of Opportunity, defend our students, and watch my back in the course of this lawsuit.

So, while my advice is to avoid lawsuits, we cannot avoid telling the truth. "The truth," urged W.E.B. DuBois, "is today, be good, be decent, be honorable and self-sacrificing and you will not always be happy. You will often be desperately unhappy. You may even be crucified, dead, and buried; and the third day you will be just as dead as the first. But with the death of your happiness may easily come increased happiness and satisfaction and fulfillment for other people—strangers, unborn babes, uncreated worlds. If this is not sufficient, never try it—remain hogs."

I decided to file this suit not so much because of what happened to me, but because the board continues to harm our students. They refused to score our TABE (Tests of Adult Basic Education) tests. They refused to allow our GED graduates to participate in the citywide formal graduation ceremony.

My lead attorney, David Gespass, Southern Regional Vice-President of the National Lawyers Guild, has worked hundreds of hours, so far without pay, in my behalf. We have received financial support for court costs from the Southern Poverty Law Center. Also, the civil rights law firm of Chestnut, Sanders, Sanders, Pettaway, Campbell, and Albright from Selma, Alabama, and Wythe Holt, a professor of law at the University of Alabama, in Tuscaloosa, are co-counsel on this case.

The truth has come out and I feel vindicated regardless of the legal outcome. In depositions, board representatives have admitted that 522 students were administratively withdrawn (i.e., involuntarily). They admit the number is alarming. They have agreed that pregnancy or illness does not indicate a "lack of interest." They said far fewer students were pushed out the following year, but I am not privy to the exact number. The board set up a "dropout and recovery" program and claim they take this issue more seriously as a result of these allegations. As a settlement to the lawsuit, I have proposed to the board that they stop using the term "dropout" to describe our students. The term blames the victims and denies the culpability of the school system. I have met and worked with over a thousand adult education students and I have yet to meet a single student who woke up one morning and consciously chose to leave school. My experience has been that the school system left them. Whether it is poverty or the drive to raise test scores, both of which leave students with a sense of low self-confidence and low self-esteem, they continue to feel coerced and pushed out of school.

What happened to the 522 pushed-out students is what standardized testing inevitably leads to. The tests become the subject of education, and the students become the objects. This completely reverses the role of education. There is an antistandards resistance movement gaining strength in different parts of the country, in different districts and different classrooms, and in many different ways, but the message is the same: tests and achievement test scores don't tell us much about a human being. The official school records of our students indicate that they "lack interest." The *deeds and accomplishments* of many of our students indicate that they are going to be humane leaders as they assume their roles in this community and this world. They will achieve in spite of a system that has taken the creativity, imagination, wonder, joy, and laughter out of education, and replace it with a test system of class and racial profiling that sorts out our youth and deprives them of their innocence, while at the same time curtailing their potential. So, it is with numerous success stories that we rejoice for the "lack of interest" that thrives within the walls and within the hearts and minds of our students and staff at the World of Opportunity.

Ultimately, where we all gain our greatest strength is from our students. Their resiliency, tenacity, perseverance, and burning desire to continue their education is what motivates all of us to work in this field. They are the true voices of courage.

Steve Orel is director and lead instructor at the World of Opportunity program, a student at University of Alabama at Birmingham School of Education, and a longtime member of the Birmingham Human Rights Project. To contribute books, send donations, and support the pushed-out students, please contact Orel at World of Opportunity, c/o M.W.W., 7429 Georgia Road, Birmingham, AL 35212. Tel: (205) 271-9532. Fax: (205) 592-3725. Email: ShopMathEdu@aol.com. Tax-deductible contributions can be made payable to the 501(c)(3) nonprofit: World of Opportunity.

2

We're Here, We're Queer, Would Everyone Please Take a Seat Now So We Can Get Started?

WENDELL RICKETTS

"EVERYBODY KNOWS YOU CAN'T BE GAY AND BE A TEACHER." OR SO thought Wendell Ricketts as a freshman at the University of Hawaii in the mid-1970s. When he found someone who was both, he wrote to him, hoping for insight into how the unthinkable could be put into practice.

Fifteen years later, when Ricketts began his first professional teaching job at a juvenile detention center in Albuquerque, New Mexico, he developed a new understanding of just what it meant to be a gay teacher and of the courage it required. How important a part of his identity would being gay become for those who employed him—or for those he taught?

What he found was that his work with students traditionally considered at the margins illuminated the commonalities that form the core of human existence, no matter the differences in social class, politics, or sexuality that mark us as separate. Ricketts has set the standard for all educators, gay or straight, and his poignant lessons in tolerance will indelibly mark those who have the good fortune of calling him "Teacher."

My first semester of college had barely ended in early 1977 when Anita Bryant's "Save Our Children" campaign began making headlines across the country, vowing to stamp out lesbian and gay people in the process. (The law that prevents Rosie O'Donnell from adopting her foster children in Florida, for example, is a twenty-five-year-old remnant of Bryant's campaign.) I still remember where I was and what I was doing the night the results of the Dade County vote repealing an ordinance prohibiting discrimination against gays came in—the first time, but by no means the last, when I felt my very existence was subject to public referendum.

The following year, inspired by Bryant's success, California Senator John Briggs sponsored Proposition 6, an initiative designed to purge lesbian and gay teachers, as well as anyone "advocating the homosexual lifestyle," from every public school in the state. It was hateful, but hardly *unexpected*. After Anita Bryant, everyone knew you couldn't be gay and be a teacher.

For my part, I took some comfort in being a marine biology major; I doubted anyone would ever have a reason to make a fuss over gay marine biologists. Still, there was a way in which no choice felt entirely safe. When I came out to my mother, she had worried that being gay meant I would lead a more difficult life. Now, I worried about it, too. And that is why, when a friend offered to put me in touch with her gay uncle in San Francisco, I wrote to him immediately.

What I needed, I thought, was someone older, wiser, and more experienced (he had, at that time, reached the hoary age of thirty-seven) to answer my questions about what it meant to be gay and how a person managed it. But the uncle in San Francisco offered the extra attraction of being that mythic creature, a gay schoolteacher. The fact that he was doing what seemed undoable elsewhere only proved that San Francisco was what everybody said it was: Oz.

Though our correspondence lasted for more than a year, I realize now how two-dimensionally I saw him, in the way of young people. I was curious about him, but impersonally; he was an adjective and a noun, but what interested me most was the adjective. Still I managed, in my letters to him, to observe that it must have taken him a lot of courage to work as an openly gay teacher. He didn't jump at the chance to be falsely modest. He wrote,

> People ask me all the time whether it's safe to be gay at school, or whether they should come out. I tell them, if you let people know who you are and what you're about, whatever that is, someone's always going to hate you, so there's no guarantee of safety anywhere. What I say to other teachers is that they should watch and see what happens to me, because so far I think I'm doing pretty good. But one thing I know is that people don't come out because it's safe, they come out because the alternative hurts too much or costs too much, and then it isn't being brave, it's just being alive.

At the time, I failed to grasp the nuances of his message. Years later, after I had moved to San Francisco myself and was in the thrall of my zealous period, I dated a high-school wrestling coach and found it impossible to be sympathetic to how deeply he lived in the closet. "You don't understand," he would say. "I'm in the locker room with them. Nobody in this world would believe me if I tried to explain that I was there as a coach and not as a pervert."

He was right—I didn't understand, and I wouldn't understand for more than fifteen years, when I began my first real teaching job at the juvenile detention center in Albuquerque, New Mexico. When I walked into the boys' living area to visit a student who was on restriction or to tutor one of our GED students, I found myself narrowing my focus to a pinhole, doing my best to see nothing to the left or to the right and no more than a few feet in front of me. The unit was more or less a vast open space, with waist-high cinder block partitions around the shower area and no doors; the bathrooms were in plain view. Two rows of individual cells lined a dark hallway that ran to the back. If I went into one of those tiny cells to get away from the constantly blaring television or the noisy Ping-Pong competitions, the only place to sit was on the bed. I couldn't bring a chair to sit on because the units had no chairs that weren't bolted to the floor. I chose instead to flop down in the doorway, sticking one leg out into the hall to prop the door wide open. I took these precautions not because I worried about "temptation," but because I understood that my intentions and my character would, in a crisis, be entirely beside the point.

It isn't accurate to say that I spent the whole time at the detention home worrying about what other people might think, but it is fair to say that I was never unmindful of the possibility that someone might view my presence with a malign eye, might snicker behind his hand—or worse. What I noticed was that the women teachers (several of whom were lesbians) went wherever they needed to go. When they came onto the boys' units, they simply called out their names first—"Ms. Valencia is coming in!"—and the boys who cared covered themselves up. But the men virtually never went onto the girls' wing. If they did, they took a female teacher or guard as an escort, and she ran ahead and warned everyone before the men made it through the first security door. There was no formal policy requiring escorts, so I went alone to visit both male and female students, never feeling entirely confident that I would finish my business in either place without being challenged.

Early in my time at the detention home, one of the straight male teachers offered me some advice—he wanted to warn me against touching or hugging the female students because it might be misconstrued. "It's a lot easier with the guys," he said. "You can give them a hug, a pat on the back, or squeeze them on the shoulder. No one thinks anything of it."

What he meant by "you," of course, might or might not have included me; I hadn't come out to him yet. If I had, I'm sure his comments would have been less casual, because "no one thinks anything of it" does not exactly apply, to put it mildly, to gay men and adolescent boys. I told him I wondered what was really behind such rules—was the administration worried that we would appear guilty, or did they fear we *were* guilty?

"It's probably mostly to avoid lawsuits," he said, "but it can also help you maintain your own boundaries. You'd have to be blind not to notice that some of these young women are beautiful. That's not to say you'd ever step out of your professional role as a teacher, but. . . ."

But? Was he really implying that he might not be able to trust his own "instincts" around teenage girls? Whether as a matter of policy or of custom, the facility held him to the belief that he couldn't visit female students in their housing units without an escort, and he would surely never have been allowed to enter a girls' locker room in any school in the country (unlike my friend, the wrestling coach, and unlike thousands of lesbian coaches, who slip beneath the radar by dint of the fact that the gender police are capable of registering only heterosexist binaries).

Gay people, to say it another way, go where we feel we can, not infrequently in semi-secret; and, hyper-vigilant, we mostly stay out of trouble. Straight people assume the right to go anywhere, are little mindful of their entitlements, and make a disproportionate amount of the mess, all of which strike me as reasons to monitor heterosexuals, not gay people.

But of course the underlying premise in the mixed messages regarding gender-appropriate visitation and physical affection at the D-Home (though hardly only there) was that *men's* sexuality (read: nature) is suspect, a shadow corollary of the sexist presumption that anything men do carries more weight. Gay and straight men share the privilege of that presumption as well as the burden of that prejudice, but gay men, by several orders of magnitude, are more sexually suspect. As I write, the Catholic Church has reacted to allegations regarding its toleration of child molesters in its employ by nominating two scapegoats—homosexuality and the failure of the vow of celibacy, as if the violation of children and adolescents were the tragic outcome of the slippery moral slope that necessarily inheres in being gay, or else the *faute de mieux* response of randy clerics who'd otherwise be dating adult women if only the Pope would let them. Would it be sacrilegious to pray to be spared the disingenuous disclaimers that will come when remediation based on these false causes fails to reduce child abuse in the priesthood by one single case?

Back at the D-Home, meanwhile, I did come out to my fellow teachers and to my principal, but I never deluded myself that my students would welcome the knowledge that I was gay. (National surveys show, rather consistently, that only about 60 percent of high school students say they would feel comfortable with a gay teacher.) So I did not tell my students, though I kept my promise to myself that I would neither lie nor dissemble.

One student, however, figured it out—or made a guess that turned out to be right. He was a thin, white, Eminem-looking seventeen-year-old who drew SS-style lightning bolts on his handouts. Custody staff found a note in his cell in which he talked about stabbing the fag teacher and the nigger teacher—the art teacher, a black woman—with sharpened pencils. They took him out of classes and put him on twenty-three-hour-a-day lockup for the rest of his sentence. I was told I ought to feel very lucky.

WHAT I CAN SAY IN A GENERAL WAY ABOUT BEING A QUEER teacher is pretty much what many other, more experienced and more eloquent people have already written and said (see, e.g., Rita Kissen's excellent *The Last Closet: The Real Lives of Lesbian and Gay Teachers* and resources available through the Gay, Lesbian, and Straight Education Network, online at <http://www.glsen.org>), and pretty much what anyone could figure out if she or he dedicated a few moments of thought to the subject: Being a gay teacher means entering every new workplace not certain whether it will be safe for you to be out, and not clear how you will handle things if it isn't. In many places in America, of course—many, but not most—discrimination against lesbian and gay teachers violates employment policies and is illegal. But that's different from saying that discrimination doesn't exist or isn't sanctioned. In litigious America, civil rights pretty much boil down to what you have the money and the stamina to prove in court. It's still easier to win a verdict against a fast-food chain for serving you coffee that is too hot than to show that your employer has treated you illegally. So one of the things being a gay teacher means is knowing that you are largely on your own if you are harassed by students or targeted by parents; it means that you stand a greater chance of being falsely accused of "inappropriate" behavior with your students and a smaller chance of being defended against such accusations by your school or union. Prejudice, all too often, is policy.

Being a queer teacher means that, while you may be able to attack racist and sexist language in your classroom, you will be unable to combat homophobia without exposing yourself to uncomfortably personal scrutiny. It means that you will wish you had a dollar for every time you are forced to endure the speech that begins: "I don't care if a person is white, black, brown, green, purple, gay, or Martian, I just don't think it should be shoved in my face." It means understanding that most straight people have no interest in acknowledging how relentlessly they declare their heterosexuality—wedding rings, pictures of the hubby and kids on the desk, self-deprecating tales of alimony payments and divorce, even the unselfconscious use of the correct gender pronouns when they talk about their partners. They "out" themselves constantly as heterosexual without ever uttering the word; the identical behavior on the part of a lesbian or a gay man, however, is considered "flaunting it."

Being open as a gay educator among your colleagues also sometimes means being, by default, the one "in charge" of identifying homophobic assumptions. When I supervised an adult education program for ex–jail inmates, for example, one of our women students reported to a teacher that another student, a lesbian, had made a pass at her. The teacher's immediate response was to suggest calling the two women together so the "offended" party could "confront" the lesbian student about her inappropriate behavior. A bit of investigation revealed that the "pass" involved the lesbian student patting the seat beside her and asking the other woman to "come sit next to me." The woman who complained acknowledged that the lesbian student had not been physically or verbally aggressive or lewd and that the incident had happened only once; the lesbian student acknowledged that she had been flirting. I derailed the "confrontation" session and suggested that the faculty meet as a group before we took any further action. At our meeting, I asked, "Is the problem here that our participants sometimes flirt with each other, or is it that same-sex flirtation requires special attention? Because if it's the latter, then I propose we make a new rule forbidding our students from any expression of sexual and romantic interest in each other during program hours, and I would like to hear suggestions about how we will police that."

No one, of course, felt able to determine which of our participants were sitting together at lunch for platonic reasons and which for romantic reasons, or who was exchanging phone numbers in order to offer to help with childcare and who because he or she was trying to get a date, and no one wanted to be in charge of the interrogations that would clarify matters. The result was that the direction of our discussion shifted significantly.

In another incident, a gay student with obvious mental health problems began lavishing gifts on a heterosexual male teacher. The teacher wanted the student to be counseled that "giving gifts to another man could really get you into trouble in a correctional setting." Instead, I asked the teacher to return the gifts and explain, as gently as possible, that teachers simply weren't allowed to accept presents from students, no matter how much they appreciated the kindness that lay behind the gesture.

In both cases, we had the opportunity to affirm our participants' humanity; in addition, the individual incidents meant a chance to strengthen our commitment to combating sexual harassment when it did occur and to reassert the importance of clear student/teacher boundaries. But work was required to steer the response away from the initial heterosexist impulse to decontextualize and isolate same-sex interest as inherently pathological. Not infrequently, the only one signing up to do that job is the queer educator.

BEING A GAY TEACHER, OF COURSE, IS ONLY PART OF MY STORY. As I've made clear, I also choose to work in prisons and jails, settings in which teaching is both easier and harder than in the free world. About halfway through my first day at the juvenile detention center in Albuquerque, for example, I found a small, empty room just off the deserted cafeteria, closed the door behind me, and cried for twenty minutes. The thoughts that accompanied my crying jag were hardly profound; what I repeated to myself between sniffles was a single sentence: "This is too hard." Too hard to experience the depression and resignation in the lightless eyes of the young men and women in my classroom. Too hard to balance their need for my attention with the sometimes beastly means they used to get it. And too hard, most of all, to manage my own pain, which, like some nocturnal creature, had stirred to life in recognition of my students' kindred calls.

By that point in my life, I had been involved in prison work, though not as a teacher, for more than eight years. I knew prison life as fully as you can know it without being a prisoner yourself—which is to say that I knew it secondhand. Still, I'd had a clear window into its deprivations and depredations; its thousand petty tyrannies; its desperate loneliness; the gray, relentless tonnage that it brings to bear, literally and figuratively, on the most fragile aspects of human existence, extinguishing first human connection and then, inexorably, the very desire to connect.

The most profound lesson I have learned from the prisoners I've had contact with is that I am them. I say that with no bravura, no bleeding-heart sense of over-identification, no attempt to claim experience or wisdom I didn't earn. I say it, instead, with the respectful admission that none of the groups in which I can legitimately claim personal membership—gay men, the working class, mixed-race ethnic mongrels—has given me a more profound and meaningful experience of the fragile, contingent nature of human existence than have the prisoners I've known and taught.

What I've learned from prisoners is that the only useful distinction to be made is not between those who have broken the law and those who haven't, or even between those who have or haven't been caught, but rather between those who can imagine knowing and loving (let alone being) someone who has gone to prison and those who cannot. Americans for whom such a possibility is remote beyond conception truly do stand on the far rim of a wide divide. Indeed, acceptance of the possibility that life is capable of falling apart utterly, that chaos and tragedy are neither unlikely nor even especially surprising— what I consider an important aspect of prison(er) consciousness—resonates deeply within me. And far from being the occasion for cynicism or despair, it is that knowledge, ironically, that holds me in a place where life is capable of having genuine meaning.

Above my desk, I have pinned a copy of Linda Pastan's poem, "A Short History of Judaic Thought in the Twentieth Century." In the poem, the narrator rails against the rabbinical law that to touch the dying is forbidden—except in cases in which they may be carried from a house that has caught on fire. "And whom may I touch then," demands the narrator, "aren't we all/dying?" Pastan concludes,

> You smile
> your old negotiator's smile
> and ask:
> but aren't all our houses
> burning?

People often wonder why I choose to do my teaching in correctional settings where (so they think) the students are thankless and the gains are so fleeting and so few. I rarely answer such questions directly, preferring to let people believe, as they will, that I am either some kind of saint or else the teaching profession's equivalent of the perennial underachiever. The truth is that I have two clear motives, which I mainly keep to myself.

First, I believe that teaching is—or properly ought to be—political work. At the same time, I believe that prisons are the physical manifestation of the bluntness of our responses to human rage, disillusionment, and thwarted need, the symbol of our bottomless willingness to commit waste. They are a monument to dysfunction, and their legacy of failure implicates individuals, systems of government, and entire nations alike. Differences are a matter only of scale. Thus, when I work in correctional education, I struggle against the oppression of my fellow human beings, and I am challenged to resist the insidious urge to reproduce systems of oppression in the classrooms and programs over which I have authority.

But there is also a second reason. It is that like me—but also in a thousand ways I can't even begin to imagine—my students live in houses that are burning. When I touch them and they touch me, when we do our best to carry each other away from the fire, it is because the alternative costs too much and it hurts too much. And that isn't being brave, it's just being alive.

Wendell Ricketts is Supervisor of Education at the San Francisco Sheriff's De-partment's Post-Release Education Program. Ricketts is author of Lesbians and Gay Men as Foster Parents, *published by the University of Southern Maine in 1991, and his articles, fiction, and poetry have been published in numerous mag-azines and anthologies. For his work translating the plays of Natalia Ginzburg from Italian, he was awarded the PEN American Center Renato Poggioli Prize for 2000, and his poem, "Elegy for Matthew Shepard," was nominated for a 2000 Pushcart Prize.*

3

The Monster in Our Schools

TERESA GLENN

It didn't occur to me that . . . you can get in trouble for . . . discussing the shortcomings of these tests, particularly when they are almost life and death—at least academically—for these students.

I know we talk about high standards, but in my mind just teaching kids to answer multiple-choice questions is about the lowest standard I can imagine. That's not the same thing as having the skills to live a productive life in a democratic society. I think we're robbing students of what education should be about, which is a love of knowledge. . . .

—North Carolina teacher Teresa Glenn
on the public radio program "This American Life"
November 3, 2000

*A*bout forty-five minutes into the End of Grade test, Eli raised his hand. "Ms. Glenn, I can't figure this question out. I've been looking at it for ten minutes and I can't get it."

That was it. That one difficulty started it all—a student's frustrated plea for help during one of the most important days of his academic career. As a result of that exchange, I found myself the object of an inquiry by the North Carolina Department of Public Instruction, my school board, the superintendent, and my principal. Before the dust settled, I had been threatened with being fired, having my license revoked, and being banned from teaching in my state.

I don't want to start with that melodrama, however. I want to start with my students. I arrive at school every morning because of them—not because the administration says I have to and not because of my paycheck. It's the kids' gravity that pulls me back; it's the kids' ideas that force me to stretch myself; it's the kids' desire to understand that compels me to teach. The kids fuel me.

The students that year were challenging—intellectually, emotionally, in every way you can imagine. I joined them in November, six weeks after the previous teacher left. Although I was trained as a high school English teacher, I had taken a job teaching eighth grade the January before. As it turned out, eighth grade seemed to be my niche. The students lacked an internal censor and freely discussed everything from personal hygiene to their parents' fights; they would argue any point until they'd forgotten what the initial argument was about; they rudely pointed out pimples, bad hair days, breakups with boy- or girlfriends, and clothing from unacceptable stores. But at the same time they wrote notes to me begging for extension of projects with the notation "WB" (write back) at the bottom; they obsessed over the smallest details of their attire, seeking approval of a new hair clip from their friends; they had impressive collections of gel pens and were likely to write on notepads featuring Hello Kitty or Winnie-the-Pooh. I was hooked. When the job opened up at a strong middle school in an area where my family and I wanted to live, I took it.

I did not realize that after six weeks with substitute teachers, I would have to be part lion tamer, part professional wrestler to accomplish anything with the kids. Bright, funny and very, very stubborn, they tested me at every turn—losing books, turning in assignments late, pretending not to understand directions, and (the bane of all teachers) asking silly questions for the benefit of a giggling audience. Martin, who should have gotten a paycheck for the entertainment value he added to the class, took every opportunity to ask penetrating questions such as, "Ms. Glenn, what kind of music do you listen to?" and "Ms. Glenn, who's your favorite TV star?" Martin's questions usually arose during vocabulary lessons or discussions of the grading of a project. Megan and Elizabeth made sure to stay after class to share gossip about who was going out with whom—both students and teachers. Vince, knowing that he was far more intelligent than I, argued for the sake of arguing, and frequently revisited arguments that had been previously resolved. They were smart, funny, and they required every ounce of energy and passion that I had. By Christmas, however, the students and I had bonded and I settled into a routine with them. We'd worked out the major kinks in our relationships (Martin was allowed three comments per class, Megan and Elizabeth could only talk about their own social lives, and Vince could reargue his cases only if he brought in extra facts or readings to support his opinion the second time around).

There were a couple of students who stood out right away; Eli was one of them. He'd built a reputation as a smart, conscientious student. His mom was a teacher at the rival middle school. A good friend of Vince's but lacking Vince's penchant for debate, he stayed quiet during discussions, preferring to come in at odd times, make a quiet but relevant comment, and then return to listening mode. But his comments nearly always interrupted the flow of the discussion, introduced a new element that hadn't been present before.

That's why Eli's confusion on that year's End of Grade (EOG) test was so surprising. The EOG tests are used in North Carolina to make promotion decisions about third, fifth, and eighth graders. All students in grades three through eight take them, but only those three grades must pass the test or face retention. The EOG tests are given in math and reading and take three days of testing to complete. Schools post their EOG results on the signs on the front lawn; my school had a banner in the front lobby proclaiming that we had been a School of Distinction in years past. Teachers are called out by name in faculty meetings where the scores of their students are discussed, and school rankings are published in newspapers. Students receive plaques at awards ceremonies for scoring level fours (the highest score) and others receive ice cream parties and special trips for doing well on the tests. At my school, we have instituted a special thirty-five-minute EOG test preparation period every day, teachers are required to give multiple-choice EOG-formatted tests every six weeks, there are four different test preparation books for each teacher to use, and math and reading receive twice as much instructional time as science and social studies (those subjects are not tested). In short, the EOG tests have become the focus of much of the energy in North Carolina schools. They're the end-all, be-all for politicians, the media, and a public misled by politicians and the media.

What the EOG tests do not test is the ability to do anything beyond answering multiple-choice questions. A student who's good at taking tests can usually figure out what answer the test designer wants him to put down. Eli was a good test taker, he'd aced all the practice exams, and I knew he'd do well on the real EOG.

The frustration on his face was clear. "Ms. Glenn, I can't figure this question out. I've been looking at it for ten minutes and I can't get it."

My immediate thought was that he'd spent way too long looking at that one question. The kids have a little shy of two hours to read ten lengthy passages and answer about sixty-five questions. Ten minutes on one question was nine minutes too long.

I took the test booklet from Eli. I read the question. (Now would be the time in this tale where I recounted the question for you. However, since I would like to continue teaching in North Carolina and prefer to do so with my license, I'll refrain from paraphrasing the test question. That's what eventually got me into trouble.) I read the passage. I read the question again. I could not find the answer.

"Just go on and do the others, Eli," was all the advice I could give him.

I returned to the table in the front of my room where I'd already collected some test books from kids who were finished. I looked through the book and returned to the question that stumped Eli. The information the question asked for was not in the passage. It just wasn't there. Think of it like this. You read a passage about, say, how the days of the week got their name. Then the test question asks you what day Father's Day falls on. That information isn't in the passage, but you might happen to know it from life. In order for a kid to answer the question correctly on this EOG test, she'd have to have the answer already in her brain—she couldn't get it from what was provided in the booklet.

Then Madison raised her hand. "Can I have a calculator, please?"

Students aren't allowed to use anything but pencils and scratch paper on the reading EOG, so the question caught me off guard. Madison's also a smart kid and she should have known this as well as I did. "For what?"

"I can't figure this question out without a calculator," she said and looked up at me with fear and puzzlement in her face. "I thought this was a reading test, not a math test!"

Again, I looked at the test question, looked at the passage. (Again, I'd like to tell you what the question was, but self-preservation learned the hard way prevents me from doing so.) Question, passage. Question, passage.

Seeing my confusion, Madison tried comforting me, "It's okay, Ms. G, I'll just skip it and go on."

I went back to my table and looked at this question. It required kids to calculate numbers to the hundreds decimal place in four separate problems. I worked it out, but it took me about five minutes to do so.

By now, my activities had caught the eye of my proctor. Brenda Haywood was a member of the school board and parent of one of my students. "What's wrong?" she asked.

"I think there are two bad test questions," was my reply. "I can't figure them out—look, this one you can't answer using the passage and on this one there's a bunch of math the kids are supposed to do without calculators."

She looked at me in surprise, then looked at the questions herself. "What are you going to do?"

"I don't know. Should I file some kind of appeal or objection with Mrs. Pennington?" Mrs. Pennington was our test coordinator and assistant principal.

"I guess you should," Mrs. Haywood said.

I spent the last thirty minutes of the EOG test period writing up the inconsistencies and problems with these two questions. I also went through the entire test and looked at each question to see if there were other bad questions. When I turned in my tests—there's a rigorous counting and recounting process one must undergo each time the tests are given—I turned the sheet in to Mrs. Pennington. She placed it on a shelf in the workroom and turned her eyes to the next teacher coming in to count tests.

That evening, I logged on to my email account. The Internet has been my most valued way of interacting with other teachers and at that time I was subscribed to a listserv sponsored by the NC Department of Public Instruction (DPI). The listserv was designed for teachers and administrators to share ideas—and, in fact, it's how I got the teaching job at this school. My teaching partner at that time had posted the opening to that list.

My mind was still on the frustration and the wasted time my students had experienced during the day's test session. As I scanned my email, I noticed a post by another teacher asking for thoughts on the NC writing tests and their importance in a school's overall EOG ranking. The email touched a nerve with me. I'd just witnessed my kids struggle through a test that had at least two unfair questions on it. Those two questions represented the difference between passing and failing. The time spent struggling with those questions could prevent the kids from having enough time to finish, and it certainly would distract them from the subsequent questions they tried to answer. I fired back the following email:

[Please note: I have had to sanitize the content of the EOG test questions mentioned.]

I'm afraid you touched a raw nerve with me. For the past several months I have immersed myself in every possible book, article, website, whatever about standardized testing. The more I read, the more appalled I am at NC's [North Carolina's] testing program. What follows may be disjointed because I have numerous concerns about these monsters. Nevertheless, here are my thoughts:

First of all, the EOG tests haven't ever been validated for use in making individual assessments of students. There's no accountability for the makers of the tests, there's no check on their validity—and the testing specifications aren't released to the public. I don't think it matters, really, WHAT the various tests are weighted: how about facing the fact that these tests have NEVER been validated for the uses to which they are being put. How about facing the fact that while DPI [Department of Public Instruction] is having a grand old time "policing" the schools, no one is policing DPI.

I have emailed five different people at DPI (and none have sent me the information I requested regarding test specifications), read all the state laws & DPI administrative code—and not even the standard error is published anywhere. Teachers and the public have a RIGHT to know how these tests are created, what criteria are being used to select questions and what questions students across the state are getting right or wrong. This year on the 8th grade EOG in reading, there were two questions that were brought to my attention by my students. One asked for information not contained in the passage... [the necessary information] was *nowhere* in the reading. The other required the student to do computations (and set up the computations properly)—on the *reading* test, mind you.

...these tests are a disservice to our students—whether they count 80 percent, 100 percent, or 40 percent. The writing test is a completely artificial situation with completely artificial parameters. Bottom line: it's not reality. We write because writing is meaningful for us, it serves some purpose for us that is important. I never sit down and answer a random question like "What's your favorite class?"—and time myself... Does anyone?

I also never read anything and then answer ten multiple-choice questions about it. Call me crazy. I usually read things and then either use the information, talk about it, write about it or read something related to it. And oh yes, I have time to process the information. (Imagine that.)

...I apologize if anyone is offended by any of the above. I am personally offended by the EOG tests. I've seen students—good students, A/B students—CRYING because of these tests. I have seen students retained who work hard but lack the native intelligence to pass a two-hour multiple-choice test. I've seen teachers do nothing for the last 6–10 weeks of school but work on EOG preparation. I've seen teachers publicly humiliated because they had lower test scores than the year before. I have seen children made fun of, called names and put down based on their EOG scores. I've seen teachers look down their noses because a child is a 3/3 and not a 3/4 on the EOGs. The entire spectacle is disgusting.

In a post two days later, I got a lot more specific about the bad test questions.

One reading selection dealt with X. One of the accompanying questions asked about X. The word X appeared nowhere in the text the students read. Unless they already possessed this knowledge, there was NO WAY for a student to answer this question.

...I wonder if DPI's reluctance to release tests is because they know just how horrendously bad the tests themselves are. We retested our students with a released test and I took it with them. On five questions I couldn't be sure of the answer. Three questions required knowledge outside the reading passage (like the X question I described above). Another 5 were so poorly worded that I had no idea what the question was asking. In short, 18 of the 65 questions were themselves questionable (that's 28%—almost a THIRD of the test!).

(In case you're wondering about whether or not I'm a dummy who couldn't answer the test questions in the first place: I attended the School of Science and Math, University of North Carolina-Chapel Hill, was a Teaching Fellow and a National Merit Scholar. I know standardized tests, I've taken plenty, and this was one of the worst in terms of just plain bad questions I've ever seen.)

The other question I have is about the relative difficulty of the various grade levels of the test. I teach 8th grade. . . . I'm teaching 5th grade summer school this summer, and in looking through the 5th grade Competitive Edge EOG preparation book, I've noticed that a good number of the 5th grade practice readings are IDENTICAL to the readings in my 8th grade books! Surely reading about Oliver Cromwell isn't required in the 5th grade—but the same passage is in both the 5th and 8th grade books. . . . Are the tests this close in difficulty as well?

It seems to me that we're holding kids accountable, schools accountable, teachers accountable—but no one's examining the test and holding DPI accountable for accuracy, reliability and validity. Independent analyses of the tests need to be run. They need to be validated for making individual decisions regarding students—something DPI has NEVER done. (They have only been validated for making judgments about entire schools or school systems—NOT individual students.) They need to be reviewed by the public. DPI needs to be held accountable too.

Two days after this second email, May 30, 2000, my principal called me into his office. Mr. Wolff played college basketball and when he towers over me, it feels as though he's double my 5′ 3″ height. The interrogation was quite simple.

MR. W: Did you write an email about testing to a DPI listserv?
ME: Yes.
MR. W: What did it say?
ME: I talked about some bad test questions and about how the tests themselves are bad for students and teachers. Why?
MR. W: Someone on the listserv turned you in to DPI. They want to pull your license. The school board wants to fire you. You're meeting with the superintendent tomorrow.

After some discussion, it was clear that DPI felt I had breached the Code of Testing Ethics, a four-page insert in our test administrator's manual, that prohibits NC teachers from talking about specific test questions (and a host of other things). Paraphrasing test questions—which is what I had done—wasn't mentioned in the testing ethics. Not only were my emails with test questions paraphrased forwarded to DPI, all of my other postings blasting the EOG tests were forwarded. Seemingly I hadn't just mentioned test items, I'd asked my own questions about the tests and their validity and that's what got everyone riled up.

Mr. Wolff was very clear that DPI was gunning for my license and that, in their opinion, I ought not to be teaching in North Carolina any longer.

I left school that day thinking I might be fired and that I might lose the right to teach at all. At that time, my husband was a stay-at-home dad to three-year-old Clare and five-year-old Rachel. I was the only one working. Beyond the practical concerns, I was distraught at the idea of never teaching again. Teaching is who I am, it's not just what I do.

That night, I lay in bed trying to imagine what my future might look like without school. I could picture only an empty room.

There was a reprieve the following day. Mr. Wolff called me into his office again to read to me from an email sent by a testing coordinator at DPI. This email stated that DPI was handing over the determination of my "punishment" to the local school board and they recommended termination.

Along with the DPI listserv, I also belonged to an email group for test resisters. They offered guidance, righteous indignation, and feedback about my situation. Several contacted officials in North Carolina; many wrote emails of support. They put me in contact with lawyers and others in North Carolina working against the tests, and those folks were able to assuage some of my fears and tell me exactly how to handle myself.

Over the following week, I found myself staring at the basketball posters on Mr. Wolff's walls more frequently than I really wanted to. My case, such as it was, bounced from Mr. Wolff to the superintendent to the associate superintendent to the testing coordinator to nameless DPI workers and back around again. Initially, firing seemed certain. Then they decided that the Testing Code of Ethics didn't specifically preclude paraphrasing, so maybe they'd just suspend me for a few weeks. Then they decided the school board should have the final say. The superintendent would tell them I deserved two weeks without pay, just like another teacher who'd given students the writing test prompt before the test day.

And finally I was called into the inner sanctum of the superintendent, a place few enter willingly.

In that dim room, surrounded by stuffed bulldogs (the superintendent's personal mascot), I was told that he'd recommend to the school board that I receive two weeks' suspension, without pay, and that I had better feel sorry about what I'd done. I asked whether or not those test questions would be fixed and the superintendent replied, "That's none of your business."

I found out later that the superintendent had, in fact, told the school board in closed session that I should be fired—not suspended. I was saved by the presence of Mrs. Haywood, school board member and my test proctor. She recounted what she saw during the test, the frustration of the kids and how upset they had been. The associate superintendent with whom I had worked closely on several projects also spoke in my defense. The school board decided to suspend me for one week, without pay.

During these deliberations, I was not permitted in the room. I sat on a very hard, very red velvet couch just outside the door with the local newspaper reporter who covers school board meetings.

I served that suspension in the fall of 2000. My new class of students was puzzled by my week-long absence, which I was forbidden to explain by decree of the superintendent. During that week, I was interviewed by NPR's "This American Life" program about my suspension. I talked a lot about how money for schools was being spent on test prep materials rather than novels. I mentioned the way my school seemed to be increasingly obsessed with test scores and less concerned with human beings. It was a good way to spend part of that week. (I also spent a day in my daughter's kindergarten classroom and another shopping for baby things for the child I was expecting the coming March.)

The experience changed me. Not in the way DPI and the superintendent would have liked. It's made me more determined than ever to speak out about the End of Grade tests and how they injure kids. It's made me more understanding of my students and how they feel when teachers play "Gotcha!" with them. I talk to my students about the tests, tell them that they aren't fair (like many things in life), and our job is to beat them at their own game. My kids this year had a 90 percent pass rate on the EOG tests.

The Testing Code of Ethics changed as well. It now carries a specific warning against paraphrasing test questions. Violators may be prosecuted.

The End of Grade test did not change. One of the bad test items I questioned in May 2000 appeared on the eighth grade reading EOG this spring. The kids' hands went up this time, too.

Teresa Glenn, a nontenured teacher, was forced to resign from this school at the end of the 2002 term. Shortly after, she accepted an offer to teach in a charter school in Wilmington, North Carolina.

4

Science Means What We Say It Means, or, My Adventures in Wonderland

JOANNE YATVIN

As One of Fifteen People Commissioned by Congress to Serve on The National Reading Panel in 1998, Dr. Joanne Yatvin, an educator with more than forty years' experience, took this prestigious appointment seriously. She quickly became disillusioned, however, with the hurried process that resulted in the panel's narrow pronouncements about literacy. Knowing that the incomplete and flawed findings would be used to guide reading instruction for years to come, she felt compelled to write a minority report expressing her dissatisfaction with the panel's work. To date, her objections remain a largely undisseminated, unread piece of the government's official document heralded as the nation's definitive, research-based report on literacy.

I have always felt that I sneaked into teaching and school administration when no one was looking. My appointment to the National Reading Panel was another such lapse on the part of the gatekeepers. If they'd known who I was, where I'd been, and how I got from "there" to "here," they'd never have let me in.

Who was I? A whole language teacher who'd spent more than forty years in public schools learning about literacy. I had begun my career as the lone third-grade teacher in a rural school just after completing my B.A. in English, getting married, taking education courses in summer school, and moving a hundred miles away from my city home. That year, while struggling with all the problems of a beginner, I took my first course in reading. One night a week, I traveled on winding country roads to another rural school where a professor from the state teachers college inducted about twenty of us into the mysterious and joyous sorority of reading teachers.

Early in the school year, I realized that about five of my students were nonreaders and about eight more were not skilled enough to grapple with third-grade textbooks. Working with an old set of basals, most of the kids and I made progress, but we were still far from being a success story. I was sure I could do better if I were given the chance to start children out in reading, and so I sought a new job teaching first grade.

In my new classroom I had a set of fairly recent Scott, Foresman basal readers with a teacher's guide. The sight word/limited vocabulary approach worked well with these children, especially, I think, because I was tenacious. I met with reading groups twice a day and worked with the neediest children individually, going over the same stories until they had mastered them. Memory tells me that every child went on to second grade as a reader.

After three years, I left teaching to have children of my own. During that time I did some substituting in upper elementary grades and was attracted to the possibilities there. Although I considered myself a successful teacher, I was tired of the primary curriculum. I didn't want to live with Dick and Jane, workbooks, and coloring sheets anymore. I wanted to sink my teeth into content, but more important, into real books, projects, research, drama, and all that fun stuff.

Most of my succeeding experience can be squeezed into a metaphor of climbing and exploration. I tried fifth, sixth, seventh, and eighth grades, then detoured into middle school English. Along the way, I abandoned textbooks and turned to a mix of paperbacks, reference materials, and teacher-invented activities that worked a lot better for my students and kept me interested, too. My students chose their own books for reading, wrote a paper a week, and constructed personal spelling lists from words they had trouble with in their writing. When a new high school was about to open, I applied for the position of English department chair, even though I had never taught high school before, and got it. I brought most of my middle school teaching habits with me, changing only from individualized reading to having small groups read the same book because I just couldn't keep up with a hundred or more student choices. I soon saw, to my embarrassment, that students were more active and insightful in group discussions than they had been in the one-on-one conferences I had thought so valuable.

After eight years of high school teaching, I decided that I wanted to be a principal—but not at that level. Spending my days patrolling restrooms and my evenings taking tickets at sports events was not my idea of professional challenge. I applied for an elementary principalship in the same district, and, after being told by the personnel director that I wasn't qualified, I was chosen by a committee of parents and teachers.

All these job changes were made without the proper certifications. Some of my jobs didn't require a special certificate at the time. With others, I was able to take the required courses after being appointed. Although, while teaching, I had earned an M.A. in English and a Ph.D. in curriculum and applied linguistics, neither degree qualified me in the eyes of the state for secondary or administrative certification.

In many ways my professional life began when I became a principal. I found out that my real place was working with teachers and that my appetite for learning was enhanced by being freed of university course requirements. Without books to read and papers to grade for my classes, I had time to read and write for my own interests, time to go to professional conferences and become involved in professional organizations. I quickly learned how to manipulate a school budget so there was money for the things teachers really needed—and none for workbooks. I wrote grants so we could buy multiple copies of paperbacks for every grade level and put all the basals and most of the textbooks in storage. In addition, we mixed grades in all our classrooms and grouped teachers into planning teams. I scheduled special subjects so that teachers at a grade level had common planning time. I wooed or bullied parents to get their support for our school's unorthodox ways. And finally, to give legitimacy to our program, I did research studies to demonstrate successful student learning.

While a principal in Wisconsin, I won some awards, published educational articles and coauthored a book. Then, for lots of reasons, my husband and I moved to Oregon. When I applied for jobs there, I found that I needed Oregon School Law and a few other courses I hadn't taken in order to get an administrator's license. But, again, there was a way to sneak in. If a school district wanted to hire you and sought a waiver, the state would issue a temporary license and give you a year to take the required courses. One small rural district wanted me badly enough as their superintendent-principal to do just that. I joked to my family and friends that at my funeral, someone would rush in shouting, "Wait. Don't close the casket. She needs three more credits."

And so, I began again, this time with a middle school and an elementary school to manage, but with only fifteen teachers between them. My schools had problems, including growing poverty and drug use in the community and children's bad behavior at school. I was a problem, too: a Jewish city girl who didn't live in the community and who held radical notions about educating children. My strength was my teachers, who wanted better schools and were willing to work with me to get them. Together, we brought in mixed-age classrooms, Whole Language, inclusion of special education students in regular classrooms, in-school jobs for older students, and reasonable discipline. We never complained to our community that we had too few resources, and we never told any parent that it was "too late" for their child to learn. The most dramatic change we saw was in student behavior. When our alienated kids began to see that school had good things to offer them—academically, socially, and personally—they bought in and gave us hard work and good behavior in return. Without much attention, our state test scores began to rise. Although we never reached the state goals for third grade, by eighth grade, better than 90 percent of our students read at grade level, and one year our writers were among the best in the state.

That's where I was when Congress authorized the establishment of a National Reading Panel in 1997. Hoping to make some sense of the competing claims of various reading approaches and programs used in schools, Congress asked the "Director of the National Institute of Child Health and Development (NICHD), in consultation with the Secretary of Education, to convene a national panel to assess the status of research-based knowledge, including the effectiveness of various approaches to teaching children to read." NICHD was to seek nominations and appoint a panel of not more than fifteen individuals, including "leading scientists in reading research, representatives of colleges of education, reading teachers, educational administrators, and parents." From this charge, it is clear that Congress wanted a range and balance of perspectives on the panel. But that is not what they got. From more than three hundred nominations, NICHD selected nine experimental scientists, two university administrators, one teacher educator, one school administrator (me), one middle school teacher, and one parent.

I first became aware of the panel's existence in January 1998, when I received a phone call from NICHD telling me that I had been nominated and asking me if I would serve if selected. Without quite understanding what the panel was all about, I said yes. I was flattered to be considered for what appeared to be a great honor, and I hoped to be chosen. Two months later I was notified of my appointment to the National Reading Panel.

Shortly afterward, *Education Week* ran an article listing the names of the panel members and reporting reactions from various educational leaders. I did not know anyone on the panel, and only one or two names seemed familiar. However, it struck me as strange that none of the reading researchers and educators I knew of and admired had been selected. Moreover, comments from critics made me wary. They asserted that the panel had been packed with advocates of one type of research and one philosophy of reading. A friend of mine was more direct. "They'll eat you alive!" she commented. "Oh, well," I answered with a bravado I didn't feel, "They may find me hard to swallow."

The National Reading Panel met for the first time in late April at the National Institute of Health (NIH) headquarters in Bethesda, Maryland. NICHD officials were cordial, my fellow panelists were friendly, and I had no feeling of being left out. At our initial work session, various agency officials and distinguished guests lectured us about the mission of the panel and our responsibilities as members. In addition, the work of a previous committee appointed by the National Research Council (NRC) that had produced a widely disseminated report, titled *Preventing Reading Difficulties in Young Children*, was summarized by two committee members. NICHD officials emphasized that our job was to build on that earlier work by going more widely and deeply into the research on reading. The NRC committee had given the world a consensus document; ours would be an objective analysis of the entire field of scientific evidence on reading. Finally, NICHD distributed two papers about medical models for evaluating research and exhorted us to follow their lead by adopting similar high standards.

That afternoon the panel went through a whirlwind of decision making. With almost no discussion, we adopted the same three categories as the NRC committee—decoding, fluency, and comprehension—for the framework of our own review of research. In my opinion, such a structure left no room for looking at the children's social, cultural, linguistic, and literary learnings that both precede and grow along with their mechanical reading skills, and I lobbied for a broader framework. Although the panel listened politely, they did not respond to my concerns, and we moved on to other matters. In contrast, another panelist's proposal, that we include the use of technology in our reviews of research, generated a lot of discussion and was ultimately approved.

I should not have been surprised by this turn of events. My proposal would have meant accepting the validity of a model of reading that was antithetical to the beliefs of most of the members of the panel. The second proposal just involved adding a currently popular topic to the range of our investigation. Moreover, that proposal came from one of the scientists. As time went on, I saw that the opinions of the panel's scientists always carried more weight than those of the rest of us. Panel decisions repeatedly demonstrated that experience working in schools with children—mine or any other teacher's—was not highly valued. Our views were "intuitive"; theirs were "scientifically based."

When subcommittees were formed to review research in the selected categories, I volunteered for the decoding subcommittee. Its title led me to hope that the scope of our investigation might include all the components of a written code, such as print conventions and literary devices. More important, however, I hoped to be able to temper some of the enthusiasm for phonemic awareness and phonics already expressed by other members of the subcommittee. Ultimately, although I was able to soften some of the hyperbolic language in written drafts of our reports, I could not persuade the subcommittee members to consider the factors other than letter-sound relationships that go into breaking the written language code. Tellingly, perhaps, everyone started to call our group the "alphabetics" subcommittee instead of the originally designated, "decoding" subcommittee.

Between the first and second panel meetings, panel members exchanged many emails on a listserv that had been set up for our use. With time to think, many members were examining our hasty decisions more carefully. It seemed like a good opportunity to voice my concerns again and to argue them more logically and fully than I had been able to do at our meeting. So I wrote several emails trying to persuade the panel to restructure our project on a broader basis. The members who responded either argued against me or treated me like a simpleminded child. Because I believe my emails from that time speak more eloquently of my efforts than I can do in retrospect, I am including two of them in their entirety—the first and the last—and excerpts from a few of those in between. I will not edit my language, except to delete names, nor will I show any of the responses, out of respect for the privacy of the writers. However, the reader can discern pretty well from my messages what others were saying.

Date: Mon, 27 Apr 1998

[Name deleted]:

Your sacrifice was indeed noble. It helped me to get some practical handle on what I should be doing and how. I accept all your suggestions and look forward to your paper on doing a research synthesis.

On another note everyone may remember my expression of discomfort with the three areas (pillars?) of reading identified by the NRC report. It seemed off-balance and incomplete to me, but I didn't understand why. Now, I do, and I would like to share my view with you.

The three areas are not of the same weight or nature. Fluency is the result of competence in decoding, comprehension and understanding the ways language and literature work. It is the absence of language/literature knowledge as a pillar that bothers me. Real reading is looking beyond the pronunciation and meaning of words and even sentences to the forms, devices and conventions of oral and written language, how they interact and convey meaning that is greater than what is on the printed page. For example, without the intonation patterns of speech, word reading is often ambiguous and sometimes unintelligible. For another example, what sense do the words "once upon a time" make if you don't know they are a common device to begin a fairy tale?

I would like the group to consider how the language/literature aspects of reading can be given their proper importance without throwing out the agreements and organizing arrangements we have already made.

Joanne

Date: Tue, 28 Apr 1998

[Name deleted]:

I regret that you do not see the relevance of linguistic and literary knowledge to our charge. Without those considerations, we might just as well limit the teaching of reading to grocery lists.

Joanne

Date: Tue, 26 May 1998

I think [name deleted] is defining our charge too narrowly, thereby keeping out what might be valuable contributions to our knowledge. Why are we bound to three topic divisions that were selected hurriedly and almost casually at our first meeting, probably because they were the ones in the other report (that I can't think of the name of right now)?

It seems to me that if any member of the panel believes there is a significant body of research in any area that has an impact on the teaching of reading, we should include it in our consideration.

Joanne

Date: Wed, 3 Jun 1998

Everyone:

. . . I believe strongly that you can't pick up a teaching program—no matter how effective it appears under experimental conditions—and plunk it down in a classroom or school without regard for the unique conditions of that environment. The only people who are in a position to know these conditions are the teachers and the principal on site. For better or worse, they must have some latitude to choose the methods, materials and support services to be used. . . . Prescribing methods, materials, and/or teaching scripts will not solve the problem . . . Ultimately, I hope that teachers, principals and curriculum directors will be able to select, create or adapt classroom reading programs that embody those components without any legislative body deciding that "one size fits all."

Date: 6 Jul 1998

To the National Reading Panel:

Since our first meeting as a panel, I have expressed concern about basing our literature search on the categories of the alphabetic principle, comprehension and fluency. These categories were the ones used in the NRC report, which we adopted without much discussion or reflection. My objection, then and now, is that they cannot give us complete and balanced coverage of the research on reading. By treating these three categories as if they were the foundations of learning to read, we will omit or undervalue knowledge of print conventions, the relationship of oral language to written language, and the structure of texts. We will also give fluency more attention than it deserves, ignoring the possibility that it may be merely a result of other skills; and give comprehension less because the overall term masks the large array of skills that goes into comprehending any text. Moreover, we will deny literary knowledge a place among the pillars of reading, relegating it to secondary importance among the content areas, to be addressed only after one has learned to read. (I am talking about knowing The Three Little Pigs, not Beowulf.)

My concerns have not been addressed, and the panel has proceeded on its original course almost to the point of no return. Because I do not wish to be placed in the position of having to dissent from the final report because certain areas of research were not even explored, I request once more that we broaden our search. Since subgroups and individual members have already begun their work in the selected categories, I cannot now ask that they be abandoned, however unsatisfactory I find them. But I do ask that other categories be added and given equal status. They are: print conventions, text structure and oral language competence (i.e., grammar, vocabulary and voice inflection) as they relate to learning to read.

In line with my concerns about the content of our literature search, I am also dismayed by the sloppiness of our decision-making process. So far, we have not used voting or consensus, but have allowed the voices that speak first or more frequently to prevail. This error needs to be corrected immediately, and a more democratic process instituted. Having accepted appointment to this important panel, we all have a solemn duty to insure its democratic operation. Moreover, if our findings and conclusions are to carry any weight among educators and the public, they must be the results of open inquiry, respectful debate and collective wisdom that we can all attest has taken place.

Joanne Yatvin

Over the next year and a half, nine panel meetings were held, with much correspondence and a few subcommittee meetings in between. On the whole, one group did not know what another was doing. Even within a group, so much of the selection and analysis of research studies was done by one or two scientists and their assistants that nonscientist members were left in the dark. Could I have contributed more to the process than I did? Yes and no. After I wrote my minority view, one panel member chided me for not taking on a topic I was interested in on my own. But I could not have done that. I lacked the expertise in statistical analysis, the time, and the technical support the panel scientists had. Still, I did suggest lines of inquiry early in the process, and, on my own, I engaged a research librarian to do a search of studies on embedded phonics instruction. She turned up a list of fifty-two studies that I submitted to our subcommittee chair, but they were never reviewed. She explained that since some incidental phonics was a part of every reading program, one could not study that component separately. Although I did not fully understand her explanation, I did not object. Throughout the panel's tenure, I deferred to the superior knowledge of the scientists when it came to research. In matters philosophical, ethical, and practical, I considered myself their equal and held my ground.

I first entertained the idea of writing a minority report at the October 1999 meeting when subcommittees summarized their findings before the whole panel. It was then I realized just how few topics had been investigated and that we would undertake no more investigations. It also struck me that some of the topics investigated were trivial in light of our charge from Congress and the needs of teachers. The product of all our labors was no more than a narrowly focused review of one type of research, but it was going to be presented to Congress and the public as the complete and definitive answer to all questions about teaching reading. Outsiders would surely assume that any topic not investigated was not worth the trouble. Feeling that I could not allow such a misrepresentation to go on without protest, I decided to dissent from the report as publicly and loudly as possible. I asked two of my fellow panel members who had expressed similar reactions to the report to join me in a minority report, but they were hesitant and ultimately decided not to. My family and friends, on the other hand, urged me on. For them, it was a simple matter of showing right from wrong.

But for me, it was never that simple. I liked most of the panel members; I respected their knowledge; I knew they had worked hard; and I believed they were sincere. I also recognized that I had come onto the panel with my own biases and was never willing to surrender them. Moreover, my experiences as a teacher had made me skeptical about the superiority of science over other forms of knowing when it comes to education. Teaching, I had come to believe, is an art, one that often must be practiced under hostile conditions with flawed tools, unyielding materials, and unappreciative audiences.

When I conveyed my intention to the panel, it elicited little reaction. Like most of my proposals and comments during the tenure of the panel, it didn't seem to matter to anyone but me. Still, over the final three months of the panel's work, I wavered considerably. I wasn't sure that what I was doing was ethical or useful. Hardest for me was rejecting the appeals for compromise from the executive director, who was a reasonable man and who had always treated me with sensitivity and respect. I kept hoping that the introduction and summary of the report, not yet completed, would present the panel's work in a truer light, so that I could back off.

Finally, two events pushed me over the line. One was the hasty and careless completion of the phonics section just as the full report was going to press, leaving no time for a critical review by the whole panel. The other was meeting teachers and researchers I knew at a professional conference. Knowing that I understood and valued their professionalism, these educators believed that the rest of the panel did, too. They fully expected the report to support their work and help them gain the respect of legislators and the public. I couldn't bear to tell them how wrong they were.

In the end, I formally requested that my minority report be included in the full report. Outside of an angry email from one panel member accusing me of duplicity in not making my position known earlier, I got no further reaction from anyone on the panel or at NICHD. Not until the eve of a Congressional hearing in April, to which all panel members had been invited, did I see the report in its finished form. My husband had come to Washington with me since I expected that no one else would be speaking to me and I did not want to be alone and forlorn. Upon checking in at our hotel, we were given a package containing the full report, a summary booklet, a video, and the press release material to be handed out to reporters the next day. In looking over those materials, we saw that the full report did include my minority report at the end on unnumbered pages, but that it was not part of the summary booklet, nor was it mentioned in the press materials. We decided to make copies of my report and hand them out to reporters ourselves. Had we not done that, it might never have come to anyone's attention.

After the presentation of the panel's report, titled *Teaching Children to Read*, to Congress, I ceased to exist in the eyes of NICHD. More than a year later I discovered that panel activities had continued and emails had been posted, but I had been excluded from both. NICHD also published a booklet for teachers, based on the panel's findings, that "accidentally" omitted my name from the list of panel members. And, although NICHD had offered to pay the expenses of any panel members who were invited to speak at various conferences, they refused to pay mine for a presentation where I appeared with another panel member. Finally, in mid-2001, when I tried to get into the panel archives on the Internet, my password was declared invalid. And when I made a direct request to an NICHD official that I be allowed access, the archives were removed from the Internet altogether, and I was told that the items I wanted were no longer available.

In my life beyond the National Reading Panel there have been side effects, both good and bad. The worst was that I had to resign from the job I loved. During the time that NRP was being organized, my elementary school district was forced to merge with its high school district and I was demoted from a district superintendent to an elementary principal. In the eyes of my new superintendent, my service on the National Reading Panel was just an interruption of normal school business. When my contract, issued by my former school board, expired in June 2000, I was told that my new contract would require me to work five half-days per week and prohibit me from attending any out-of-state events for the next three years. Since I felt I could not accept those conditions, I resigned. Although I had held my job for twelve years and was eligible by age for retirement, I sought no benefits from the district and was offered none.

The best side effect has been that I now work at Portland State University, preparing early career teachers to qualify for continuing licenses. Both my colleagues and the university administration show that they value the work I do. Running a close second is my new professional relationships with educators all over the country who have supported my stance on the NRP report. I have also been invited to speak at professional conferences, where, for the most part, I have paid my own expenses and received no honorarium.

Although friends urged me to write about my experiences on the panel, I have—until now—been unwilling to do so. I wanted to forget, and I wanted the report to be forgotten. Neither of my wishes has come true. In the two years since its publication, the NRP report has grown to mythical proportions. It has become the foundation of legislation intended to force teachers, teacher educators, and researchers to conform their practice to one officially approved way. It has been used to enrich certain textbook publishers and to exalt the reputations of a few "experts." Misrepresented and oversimplified, the NRP report has been heralded by our federal government as the final verdict on what is and is not legitimate in teaching children to read. So, again I have to speak out, this time to a wider audience than I did in my minority report, in the hope that I can give more accurate information to educational decision makers and stronger support to good teachers and good teaching. Here and in a recent article in the *Phi Delta Kappan*, I have tried to explain, as completely and honestly as I can, how the National Reading Panel failed in its mission and why its findings should not be held up as the hallmark of science. For the immediate future, I have given up any thoughts of retirement. Like Ulysses in Tennyson's poem, I am resolved to continue journeying: "To strive, to seek, to find, and not to yield."

Joanne Yatvin teaches in the Continuing Licensure Program at Portland State University. Email her at Jyatvin@worldnetatt.net.

5

Confessions of a Testing Renegade

JAMES HOPE

EDUCATION IS IN JAMES HOPE'S BLOOD. NOT ONLY IS HIS MOTHER A RETIRED teacher, but his wife has taught at the Atlanta Area School for the Deaf for the past twenty-two years. As a veteran teacher himself (in fact, Centerville Elementary's teacher of the year for 2000–2001), James Hope has the reputation of genuinely caring for his students. When his district, Gwinnett County, Georgia, paid six million dollars for a standardized test that would determine whether a child passed or failed the fourth grade, Hope knew that the outcome of one test did not accurately or fairly assess a year's worth of progress for his students. He knew that implementing such a high-stakes instrument would narrow the curriculum and almost certainly reduce formerly creative teachers to those who "teach to the test." He wasn't the only one who knew. Parents knew as well, and organized to question the effect such high-stakes testing would have on their children.

Working with these parents in an effort to expose confusing and ambiguous test items, Hope posted to the Web six such questions that had appeared on the fourth-grade exam, questions that would never be used again. The subsequent frightening series of events left Hope and his family facing interrogation, the threat of legal prosecution, and a whirlwind of publicity. Despite the incredible and devastating events of the past year, Hope continues to speak out against testing practices that harm children.

45

"*T*he Hopes are going to jail." By the time a Gwinnett County school policeman delivered this pronouncement to a set of parents in the fall of 2000, I had already been interrogated several times by school officials and told by school police that my recorded interrogation would be turned over to a grand jury. A school policeman who showed up at our home three times had already left my wife and daughter feeling violated and afraid, but the threat of going to jail was too much for Kathy, my wife. She responded by collapsing to the floor, crying in a fetal position, while I frantically called family members, looking for comfort and support to diffuse my anger.

It appeared to me that my family was going to be destroyed for my having crossed the line in the fight over high-stakes accountability; the school system was not going to let the "crime" go unpunished.

What horrendous act did I commit that caused my school system to take such aggressively punitive action against me? Here is my story.

In 1996, the Gwinnett County school system announced plans to implement a high-stakes test called Gateway that would determine if students in fourth and seventh grades would be promoted and whether tenth-grade students would graduate. In the spring of 1997, the first pilot Gateway questions were given to fourth graders in Gwinnett County. Many of the questions were ambiguous at best, but I was not too concerned, because I assumed the point of the pilot test was to weed out bad questions. Test results were not to be returned to school, so teachers were not alarmed.

In 1998, the first dry run of the test was administered. Since the test was to be given in the beginning of April, and test items would include material taught from August to June, teachers were faced with the unenviable task of rushing through an entire year's material or purposely skipping significant chunks of curricula that would not be tested on the exam. In science, language arts, and math, I made the decision to try to touch on all areas, while in social studies I abandoned westward expansion and skipped to the Civil War, because I remembered several questions on that topic from the pilot test administered the previous year.

This forced rushing through curricula was stressful and did not serve the students well. In order to finish all the science units by the beginning of April, we needed to skip doing the hands-on experiments that reinforced scientific concepts. The school system justifies this early test date in order to have partial results ready for summer school, where students who fail the Gateway are given three weeks to learn what they missed during the year, before having another shot at the test and an opportunity to avoid being retained in grade. Full-fledged "teaching to the test" had now become standard procedure in Gwinnett County Schools at the expense of thoughtful, in-depth learning.

In 1999, the district was forced by a Freedom of Information request to release results of the pilot tests, which revealed high failure rates, despite the fact that the passing rate had been set around 45 percent for the fourth-grade test. Large percentages of students in fourth, seventh, and tenth grades failed one or more sections of the exam. Little wonder that the school system didn't voluntarily release these test scores.

The public outcry was immediate. In October and November of 1999, hundreds of parents attended school board meetings, voicing concerns about many aspects of the Gateway test. Parents asked school board members how they could justify failing so many students on the basis of one test. Other questions centered on the absence of community input on such a drastic change in school board policy. Parents repeatedly asked to be shown professional research that supported such an extreme departure from accepted promotion practices, but were shown not one document.

Standard procedure for Gwinnett school board meetings is for persons wishing to address the board at the open forum section of the meeting to sign up no earlier than 6:00 P.M. When I arrived at one of one of these heated meetings at 5:30, I discovered that the sign-up sheet was already filled with names of school system employees as well as a former local newscaster whose son was employed by the system's media relations department. All of the people whose names appeared on the sign-up list before the advertised time spoke passionately in favor of keeping Gateway, much to the consternation of the large anti-Gateway crowd. It soon became apparent that despite the large parent turnout, the school board had no intention of reversing their plans to proceed with their $6.2 million expenditure.

What the school board did propose at the October school board meeting, and unanimously approve at the November meeting, was new, lowered cut (passing) scores for nine of twelve sections of the test. These new cut scores were displayed in handouts as meaningless three-digit scale scores. The handout stated that the "scaled scores are not appropriately converted to percentages." This struck me as particularly odd since teachers had been shown Gateway results as percentages on several different forms.

In a letter to parents, the school system stated that "Since students must have the opportunity of doing well no matter which form of the test they take, the number of questions a student has to get right on different forms varies from form to form because the forms do not have the same questions. For example, if a form has one or two easier questions on the test than another form, the student would have to get more right to get the same scaled score." In other words, the whole reason for not advertising Gateway scores as percentages is that one test may have "one or two questions" that are easier than those on another form. The school system was not making it clear that for each individual Gateway test, exact passing percentages can be determined and these abysmally low passing percentages have nothing to do with high standards. I was incensed that the school system was telling parents that it was "inappropriate" to show passing percentages of a test that was to be the sole determination for promotion when this percentage could easily be determined by showing the total points obtained over the total possible points for each section of the test.

In the summer of 1999, I researched high-stakes testing and found not a single study supporting high-stakes tests as an acceptable practice of promotion for young children. Later that year, aware that high-stakes testing runs counter to established research practices, and that passing scores had been lowered to the point where it was nearly impossible for any student to fail, I anonymously wrote an eleven-page paper informing parents about the flaws of high-stakes testing in general and the Gateway test in particular. I quoted current research and discussed how Gwinnett County teachers were glossing over curricula in order to teach to the test, at the expense of creative teaching. I included information received from a teacher who was trained in the summer of 1999 to grade the short-answer portion of the test: that graders were instructed to give partial credit for language arts answers that were incorrect but contained no grammar or spelling errors. The teacher told me that if the answer was completely wrong, but the student wrote "I don't know" without grammatical errors, he or she was to receive one point credit for grammar and mechanics. The subsequent year, this policy was amended; however, students still receive grammar credit for giving a sincerely attempted yet incorrect reply on the language arts section of the test. I mailed this Gateway exposé to all ninety PTA presidents in the school system.

During the 1999–2000 school year, I attended several meetings of an anti-Gateway parent group who called themselves Concerned Parents of Gwinnett (CPoG). At these meetings, usually held at citizens' homes, we talked about how best to fight Gateway. Topics included how to coordinate speakers at school board meetings, and when and where to hand out anti-Gateway flyers.

During the 1998–1999 and 1999–2000 school years I was elected my school's representative to a group called the Teacher Action Committee (TAC), which met with the superintendent each month to discuss teacher concerns. On two different occasions I explained that it was not a good idea to put an entire year's worth of curricula on a high-stakes test administered in early April. At one meeting in 2000, a teacher from another school asked Superintendent Wilbanks if schools could obtain practice questions that were worded the same way as Gateway questions. After Mr. Wilbanks responded to this request, I spoke up by saying that for the school system to develop such questions would be nothing more than blatant teaching to the test. I added that this would not be in the best interest of the kids and would serve to narrow the curricula. Mr. Wilbanks did not even respond to my comment, but after the meeting he made a point to introduce himself to me and find out at which school I taught.

During this period I made the decision to contact media outlets in an attempt to get them to report the truth about the Gateway test. I soon found out that this endeavor would be more difficult than I imagined. After showing the ridiculously low passing scores to one education reporter of a local newspaper, I realized what I was up against. She told me flatly that if she were to write a negative article about the school system, the head of media relations for the schools would call her editor and tell him not to send her to cover any more education stories. Because school officials would refuse to talk with her anymore, she would be fired for not being able to do her job.

I phoned the editor of this same paper to plead with him to publish the low cut scores. He said that if I did not go on record to verify that the scores were indeed in the 20 to 30 percent range, he would not publish the information. He said that he did not want to risk being sued for libel. I was not willing to go on record at that time, for fear of losing my job. I suggested to the editor that he simply run a photograph of material that showed the true passing percentages. He refused. When I told him it appeared that Superintendent Wilbanks had the power to control the flow of information in the county, the editor agreed that he did.

When the Gateway was administered in April 2000, it was a major media event. One headline in a local newspaper read, "Pass or Else." Teachers at my school did their best to keep the students feeling secure prior to the test, but once the kids had the test in their hands, the situation soon unraveled. The test was chock-full of questions that were worded ambiguously, or in some cases, did not measure the curricula of the county. In my class children were crying because they thought they were going to fail the fourth grade. I, on the other hand, knew that every single student would pass the test, based on the low cut scores. Research on childhood stressors states that the only thing more stressful to young children than failing a grade is the death of a parent or going blind. My students, through no fault of their own, were experiencing this stress due to a miserably written, crude attempt to "raise the bar" in the name of phony high standards. I was livid at what I recognized as child abuse.

All six fourth-grade teachers at my school wanted to speak at an open forum school board meeting to express our concerns with the test. I was prepared to state that the Gateway was the worst test I had ever seen, inadequately measuring what was being taught in the classroom. We knew that media representatives would be present at the meeting, and we thought this would be an excellent venue to get the truth out to the public. Our principal's immediate supervisor told her that if we spoke at the meeting, it would reflect poorly on her. Not wanting to get her in trouble, we censored ourselves.

As a consolation, we were granted a meeting with an area director of the school system. At this meeting, we all expressed concerns about many specific Gateway test questions. The area director acknowledged our concern about the feelings of the children but insisted she had seen specific data showing that the test was valid. She said she would relay our concerns to the county's head of testing, who would address our concerns. We are still waiting.

The week after the test was given, I posted a half-dozen questions on an anti-Gateway Internet site set up by CPoG (Concerned Parents of Gwinnett). I posted questions that either did not measure Gwinnett's curricula, or were so poorly worded that even educated adults could not establish what was being asked. I was making the point that the test was full of such questions. The questions I posted were from a version of the test that would not be administered again, and I posted them anonymously from a public library because I feared losing my job if I spoke out against the test. I was trying to get the truth out, while protecting my career. My wife, Kathy, who types much faster than I do, assisted me by typing the questions and comments.

In the summer of 1999 I campaigned for school board candidate Kevin Jennings, in her unsuccessful bid to unseat board member Mary Kay Murphy. The school system was well aware that I was part of Ms. Jennings campaign crew. On July 19, the day after Ms. Jennings lost the election, school policeman Jim Keinard came to my house, gun on hip, and handed me a letter saying I was to report to the school police station the next day to answer questions about the "theft and dissemination" of the Gateway test prior to its administration. A school administrator whom I've never met later admitted to having copied the entire test before it was administered. Copies of the test reached local media a couple of weeks before the test was given and generated a lot of attention. Many in the Gwinnett County school system are aware that this administrator was quietly allowed to resign her position.

Because I had been working so diligently behind the scenes to bring the truth out about Gateway and now feared that my actions might cost me my job, I asked Terry Thomas, an attorney working for the Georgia Association of Educators, to come along with me to the interrogation. With tape recorder running, the first question I was asked by school policeman Jim Keinard was whether or not I was a member of Concerned Parents of Gwinnett. Visions of McCarthyism ran through my mind as I wondered if the next question would be whether or not I was a member of the Communist Party. The questioning soon zeroed in on my posting of invalid questions on the Internet site four months prior. I responded that I had posted summaries of test questions. Other questions centered on whether or not I was involved in, or knew anything about, the mailing of the test to the press prior to its administration. I answered truthfully, no. After the test was stolen, school police came to my school to see if the boxes containing the tests had been opened. They learned that the boxes remained sealed, and the shrink-wrap was undisturbed. The meeting was concluded and Officer Keinard said that the contents of the audiotape would probably be turned over to a grand jury.

Driving home from that meeting was, to that point, the most depressing time in my life. Not only did it appear that my career, which I cherished, was finished, but I was also in legal jeopardy. Kathy and I discussed the possibility of moving out of state, because it appeared that my career in Georgia was finished. It was more than I was able to process at the time. We were both filled with depression and panic. In subsequent weeks, Officer Keinard and his gun visited my house two more times, including a Sunday afternoon, when we had just returned from an out-of-town family funeral. My principal had informed the school system that we were attending the funeral, and still he came.

In the following weeks I learned that I had to submit to a lie detector test. The "high-stakes" polygraph test was to be taken in another county by Special Agent Paul Loggins of the Georgia Bureau of Investigation. I arrived with the full intention of telling the whole truth, including the fact that my wife had done the actual typing of the question, but that it was completely my idea. My attorney, who had to wait outside the polygraph room, advised me not to sign anything until he got a chance to read it first. Almost immediately, Agent Loggins tried to get me to sign a form that explained my Miranda rights and also said that I was taking the lie detector test under no duress. Two things were inaccurate about this form. First, one of the Miranda rights states that I had the right to have an attorney present during questioning; however, I was informed that my attorney would not be allowed in the polygraph room. Second, the form stated that I was not taking the polygraph test under duress, when in fact I was told that I would be terminated if I did not comply. I informed Agent Loggins that I would not sign the form unless my attorney read it first. Agent Loggins responded that attorneys don't always give the best advice and that I should sign the form. I walked out of the room and showed the form to Mr. Thomas, who quickly pointed out the discrepancies to Agent Loggins. The officer responded that it was just a standard form that everyone must sign before taking a lie detector test at that facility. Mr. Thomas informed the officer that I was willing to take the polygraph exam, but that he was advising me not to sign the form. Agent Loggins turned angrily to me, pointed, and said that he was calling the school system to tell them about my decision. I did not take the polygraph exam that day.

On August 9, I had to meet with Human Resource Officer Wendell Jackson without my attorney being present. Mr. Jackson started the meeting by informing me that Superintendent Wilbanks had been very patient with me, but that I had not been cooperative. Mr. Jackson also said that that Mr. Wilbanks questioned why I needed an attorney. I told Mr. Jackson everything, including the fact that my wife had typed the questions.

The next day, the last day of preplanning week, Superintendent Wilbanks summoned me to his office, where Assistant Superintendent Charles Buchanan and Human Resource Officer Jackson were also present. The four of us sat around a large table with the ever-present tape recorder. Mr. Wilbanks began the meeting by asking me, with a wry smile, if I usually got my wife to commit my crimes for me. He made a comment that he didn't know if my family had a lot of money, and that this matter could affect my whole family. In addition to offering the opinion that my answers sounded rehearsed, Wilbanks also told me they were going to take no prisoners. It seemed to me that the motivation behind the superintendent's personal comments that day was to get me to lose my cool and react to his mean-spirited, aggressive tone. Occasionally, the other two men would interject questions in a less hostile manner in the classic good cop–bad cop scenario that is so often overdone on ten o'clock TV network crime dramas.

A short time after this meeting, a parent in the county, who was also a member of CPoG, and her husband were told by Officer Keinard that my wife and I were going to jail. The parents made an audiotape of their interrogation, which includes Officer Keinard's threat that "The Hopes are going to jail. There ain't no doubt in my mind." To say I was enraged when I heard about this is an understatement. For the school system to make a statement implying that my daughter is to be raised by someone other than her parents because I posted a half-dozen invalid, never-to-be-used-again test questions on the Internet is an outrage. A fellow teacher who lived through the unfortunate experience of having an adult son who had run into legal problems was adamant that I prepare for what was possibly coming next. She told me that I needed to get my custody papers in order, stating who my daughter's guardian is, in case the school police came to our house and arrested us. My colleague said that if our custody papers were not in order my daughter would be whisked away to child protective services. Based on the Gestapo tactics that I had already witnessed firsthand, this scenario did not seem farfetched. As recently as February 13, 2001, Gwinnett County District Attorney Danny Porter confirmed to me that the school system still has an open criminal investigation on me, based solely on my posting a half-dozen questions after the test was administered.

In mid-October, I was again summoned to the office of the Georgia Bureau of Investigation in Hall County for my lie detector test with Special Agent Paul Loggins. They were now willing to give me the polygraph examination without my signing the release form. Agent Loggins was once again adamant about the fact that no one ever took a polygraph test at the bureau office without signing the form. Apparently my status as standardized test "outlaw" warranted unprecedented special status.

My time at the bureau that day began at 10:00 and lasted until 2:30. I was allowed one fifteen-minute bathroom break. Gwinnett School Police Officer Keinard was also present at this interrogation. Before I was strapped up, at approximately 1:30, I was subjected to more than two hours of questioning. First, Agent Loggins asked me a litany of questions, with the tape recorder running. When he was finished, he acted as though the tape recorder hadn't been working the entire time. Officer Keinard mentioned that he just happened to have another tape recorder in his car, and Officer Keinard repeated all the questions.

The questioning at this meeting took on an entirely different tone. The questions now centered on whom I had spoken with about my previous interrogations. During this meeting, Officer Keinard pulled out my personal phone records and started calling out names of teachers at my school, one by one, asking with each name if that person knew I was being investigated. Officer Keinard made a big deal out of this, saying I wasn't supposed to be talking to anyone about what was going on. I told them that everyone at my school knew what was happening, due to my frequent absences from school. I didn't understand what all the fuss was about, other than that the school system was afraid I was letting people know about their abusive treatment.

Other questions focused on the specifics of CPoG meetings. The officers wanted to know where the meetings were held, who was there, and what had been discussed. I readily answered these questions about private citizens exercising their constitutional right to meet, exchange ideas, and plan how to most effectively express our opposition to school board policy—all of which are actions that I would assume do not come under police scrutiny in other sections of the country. Although I was the only school employee who ever associated with this group, many CPoG members were visited by school police. These policemen were harassing taxpaying parents whose only crime had been their vocal opposition to school board policy.

On my second attempt at taking the lie detector test, I again met with Agent Loggins. Far from being a neutral polygraph examiner, he was quite opinionated. He told me that he wouldn't have his children in my class, and that he had taken his kids out of public school because they hadn't learned anything. When he showed me another form he said I had to sign, I again mentioned that I needed to show it to my attorney. He said that if I didn't sign it, I would be looking for another job that afternoon. He shared with me three long, perverted stories for reasons I have yet to determine. One story was about a group of men who, as young boys, would routinely take *Playboy* magazines into church and masturbate. At one such session the boys had accidentally burned down the church and their deed had been discovered when they were adults. Another story centered on a man who liked to urinate on his child. The third story Agent Loggins shared with me that day centered on a boy who had denied that he had been penetrating a very young girl's vagina even though the authorities knew that he had. It turned out that, even though the young boy insisted that he had never penetrated the young girl with his penis, he later admitted that he had in fact, used his finger.

The day had certainly taken a turn toward the bizarre. Were these stories Agent Loggins chose to share with me a pathetic attempt to rattle me, or just routine Gwinnett County school system interrogation techniques of teachers who dare to question school board policy? As this surreal day played itself out, my students were again spending their day with a substitute teacher. It was obvious to me that my school system's priorities had been horribly derailed. In their desperate attempt to make a bad test look good, there were no depths to which they weren't willing to sink.

The actual lie detector test was a particularly humiliating experience. After three and a half hours, I was finally hooked up. The questions focused on whether or not I was involved in the planning and carrying out of the theft of the exam prior to its administration, and I answered truthfully, no. After the exam was concluded, Agent Loggins asked me if I had any children. When I replied that I had one daughter in the third grade, he told me that children were cruel and they would make fun of her for what I had done. Before I left, Agent Loggins tried to get me to sign a form saying I took the polygraph test under no duress. I refused, citing the comment he had made earlier in the day regarding my having to look for another job that afternoon. As we parted ways, Agent Loggins was once again visibly angry.

The next chapter in this seemingly endless harassment involved the school police calling in for questioning every teacher whose name appeared on my phone records. The first teacher to be called in was family friend Lori Allen. At my previous interrogation by police officers, I pleaded with them not to call in Lori. I told them that she knew nothing of my test question posting, and that she had recently found out that her son was terminally ill and didn't need the stress of an interrogation. However, the school police contacted her the next day. Citing the many phone calls between her house and mine (she and my wife are also friends), Officer Keinard made mention of what he characterized as a "special" relationship between Lori and me. Lori took this not-so-subtle remark to mean that he thought we were having an affair. When she relayed this story to me, she was infuriated at being humiliated in this way. Referring to my test question posting, Officer Keinard asked Lori if she knew that I had already admitted to committing a crime.

Besides several other teachers being called in for questioning, all of them having to get a substitute teacher to cover their classes, a friend not even employed with the school system was asked to come in for questioning. He refused. A close friend of my wife, who at the time was employed as a school bus driver, was called in and had to comply since she was a school system employee. The first question they asked her was if she was a member of CPoG. She told them that she didn't understand the question. She was then asked specific questions about other friends who appeared on my phone records but were not employed by the school system.

All of these police actions took place, yet the school system is on record as saying they don't conduct criminal investigations. Assistant Superintendent Buck Buchanan stated in a November 11, 2001, article in the *Atlanta Journal-Constitution,* "We conduct our own investigation, but to be a little more objective, leave the criminal aspect up to other agencies." If this is true, how was it that my lawyer was allowed to be present at my first interrogation if it was not a criminal investigation? And how and why did the school police confiscate my phone records? The county district attorney has verified that the school police still have an open criminal investigation on me based solely on the fact that I posted the questions.

A month later I was again called in for an interrogation at the central office on the day before Thanksgiving break. This meeting was with Human Resource Officer Jackson and Assistant Superintendent Buchanan. Mr. Jackson spoke first by admitting, unbelievably, that he didn't know what the purpose of the meeting was. My students were again with a substitute teacher, while I sat at this purposeless meeting. Mr. Jackson said that Mr. Wilbanks still thought I was being untruthful and was considering an array of disciplinary action, including termination. I responded that if Mr. Wilbanks had anything on me he would have skipped the multiple interrogations and pressed charges against me. I let them know that I was tired of being threatened, and I was tired of school policemen showing up at my door with guns. I told them that the questions I posted on the Internet did not measure the curriculum and that I tried to communicate this information through proper channels at a school board meeting but was denied permission. I let them know of the cruel position students were put in, and that some of them had been crying because of poorly worded questions. I told them that putting students in such a situation is child abuse. This meeting ended up being my last with school officials.

In January 2001, and again in September of that year, I requested and was granted permission to testify in front of two Gwinnett County grand juries about the Gateway test. Besides issuing criminal indictments, grand juries in Gwinnett County investigate large expenditures of taxpayer money and issue nonbonding opinions of those expenditures. These opinions are then reported in local newspapers at the conclusion of jury members' six-month term. After Superintendent Wilbanks testified to one of the grand juries during the summer of 2000, jury members wrote in their summation that Mr. Wilbanks was "general and evasive" in his testimony regarding the Gateway test. After reading this report in the paper, I decided to make written contact with the grand jury, requesting to testify. I am not permitted to divulge my testimony on the Gateway test but I can report that neither grand jury issued a statement that I was general or evasive in my testimony. During 2001–2002 three consecutive grand juries recommended that the Gateway test should be discontinued.

In a written response to the grand jury's charges that he had been evasive in his testimony, Superintendent Wilbanks stated, "The 2000 Gateway scores showed improvement over the pilot results, as we predicted, thereby validating the reliability of the tests." However, in a response to a parent's request, dated October 6, 2000, a school official wrote, "At this time Gwinnett County Public Schools does not have the data you request regarding item reliability or validity for the 2000 administration." Which is it? Did they have validity and reliability data or not?

In February 2001, I was notified that I would receive a written reprimand for posting the questions. My attorney told me that if the school system had plans not to renew my contract, I had to be notified by April 15, a full year after the posting. April 15 came and went without incident, but on April 17, I received a certified letter from the state's Professional Standards Commission that because of a complaint filed by the school system, they were now investigating my action for possible sanctions against my teaching certificate. When my principal called Assistant Superintendent Buchanan about this development, he assured her that it was no big deal—that the school system made two or three such issuances a month and that it was standard procedure.

On a Saturday afternoon in August, while relaxing alone at home, I noticed the mail truck pull up the driveway and the mailman walk toward the door. I instinctively knew this was news regarding my certificate status, and I hoped this registered letter would be good news, that my persecution would finally be over. To my shock and surprise, the letter, which said that my teaching certificate was permanently revoked, pending appeal, was instead the beginning of another terrible chapter. I read and reread the letter in utter disbelief. When Kathy returned home and I told her about the contents of the letter, she fell apart again. It felt as if our lives had been reduced to a recurring nightmare that would not play itself out.

The school system's bizarre behavior was not limited to teachers. Parent and friend Tanya Decant, whose fourth-grade daughter passed the Gateway exam, was curious to see how Gateway was scored. Before she could see her daughter's graded exam, she was forced to sign a nondisclosure form agreeing not to talk about any of the questions with anyone. At one point when her husband, Chuck, asked to see the test, a school official told him that he was not permitted to talk, even to his wife, about the test questions. When Tanya received conflicting explanations on how a specific question was graded, she called a representative from test-maker CTB McGraw-Hill for clarification and was told that both previous explanations were inaccurate. At a monthly school board meeting, Tanya openly discussed this dilemma, as well as a concern she had about a test question her daughter told her about that did not measure the curriculum. Because she talked specifically about a Gateway test question in this public setting, she received a phone call the next morning from the head of the county's testing section, who told her that Mr. Wilbanks had instructed her to call Tanya to let her know that she would not be allowed to see her daughter's test again, because she had violated the nondisclosure agreement. Tanya was also informed that a school policeman was on the other end of the phone.

The Gateway confidentiality form that teachers had to sign before the 2001 and 2002 test administration was quite different than the one I signed in 2000. It said, in part, that Gateway material was not to be shared with any audience or "be shared, replicated, or posted by any device or article." It went on to say any violation of these terms would be considered theft of a trade secret punishable by "imprisonment for not less than one year nor more than five years, and by a fine of not more than $50,000." What is particularly ironic about this degrading threat is that no teacher, regardless of how unscrupulous, would ever bother to copy, with intent to cheat, a test whose passing scores are so low. The only motive for a teacher to ever discuss or share information about Gateway questions is to show the public how inadequate the test is and how taxpayers' money is being wasted. Threatening teachers with five years in prison for discussing bad test questions is a surefire way to keep the contents of a dismal test secret.

In the spring of 2001, I contacted and subsequently met with Atlanta-based WSB TV investigative reporter Richard Belcher regarding problems with the Gateway test. Besides showing him evidence that passing scores on the test were as low as the 20 to 30 percent range, I presented to Mr. Belcher evidence that roughly 80 to 100 percent (depending on the school) of students who passed the tenth grade Gateway did so with "minimal" passing scores. In a September 2000 press release, the school system touted that 92.6 percent of students passed the tenth-grade test, while conveniently failing to mention the overwhelming "minimal" passing scores. Reporters at the *Atlanta Journal-Constitution* were not even aware of the large percentage of minimal scores that were excluded from the press release until I brought it to their attention. I provided Mr. Belcher with enough information to do a scathing three-part whistle-blower investigation on the Gateway test that was aired in May of 2001.

Despite the obvious flaws with the test, at the May 2001 school board meeting, board members voted unanimously to approve 3.2 million additional dollars for Gateway expenditures, bringing the total price tag to 9.4 million dollars. That same evening, board members also approved a measure that raised property taxes for county homeowners and no doubt helped cover the cost of the test.

In October 2002, third- and fifth-grade students in the county were scheduled to take the OLSAT cognitive abilities test. Superintendent Wilbanks sent the chief of school police, Dennis Foster, to my school to be the proctor in my room for a test my students (fourth graders)were not taking. This peculiar action was taken two school years after I posted Gateway questions. This large, imposing stranger was to stand in my room for the day, while my nine-year-old students bubbled in answers on a standardized test. When Officer Foster was told that the OLSAT test was not being administered to fourth graders, he left the school.

My appeal to overturn the decision to revoke my teaching certificate was scheduled to take place on December 13, 2001, before a state administrative judge. I was allowed to continue teaching, pending the appeal. When the date of the hearing was made public, parents, former students, and staff rallied around me for support. Sixty parents and former students came to the hearing, making it necessary to set up speakers in the adjoining room to accommodate the overflowing crowd. Both my principal and assistant principal were slated to be on the witness list on my behalf, as well as four teachers and several parents. Television news as well as reporters from two local newspapers were also in attendance. My attorney, Mr. Thomas, let it be known that I had First Amendment rights to post the Gateway questions. The judge said that she was not prepared to hear a case on First Amendment rights and asked that the matter be handled through written briefs. On March 20, the judge issued a decision that my teaching certificate be suspended for six months. In her decision, the judge wrote that my acts were "no more egregious than the acts of a similarly situated educator who changed a student's score on a standardized test and whose certification was suspended for six months by petitioner." I fail to see how my action of bringing daylight to a secret, poorly written test is the same as cheating. The judge's decision got major attention from the local TV and print press, and many parents showed up at an area school board meeting to express their support of me and my actions. If my certificate is suspended for even one day, I've been told that I will be fired by the school system. Needless to say, this decision is unacceptable, and I will appeal to the state's Professional Standards Commission, who, besides being able to uphold the suspension, can still vote to revoke my teaching certificate.

In January of 2002, the school system announced that it will discontinue the social studies and science portions of the Gateway in 2003 because of the state's implementation of their own high-stakes test. Beginning in 2004, Gwinnett students must take math and language arts high-stakes tests from both the county and the state. In seventh grade, students will be taking two full batteries of tests in four subjects from the county and five batteries of tests from the state. These redundant tests will be wasting twice as much of the students' time and wasting even more of Gwinnett County taxpayers' money.

My story has yet to reach a conclusion. Parents and teachers in the county have been extremely supportive of me in my battle to speak the truth. Several letters to the editor from current and former parents as well as teachers have been published, trumpeting my ability as educator and expressing support for my actions to expose the school system's rotten test. Dr. Bill Cala, superintendent of Rochester, New York, schools, calling me his "hero" for the actions I have taken to expose the flaws of the Gateway test, submitted one published letter. An autoworker in St. Paul, Minnesota, also wrote to the paper supporting my act of conscience. On March 30, the editorial staff of the *Atlanta Journal-Constitution* ran a piece expressing their support of my actions and lambasting the school system for acting "childish" for their relentless two-year persecution of me.

I am in agreement with professional research that high-stakes testing is educational malpractice. However, I believe that even citizens who support this type of evaluation would be appalled by the way the Gwinnett County School System has chosen to go forward with its secretive testing program.

I have invested much time and energy in this battle, because I have seen firsthand how the politically motivated, phony high-standards movement is hurting children. In sixteen years of teaching, I have seen many trends come and go in education, and I have always tried to incorporate the good and ignore the bad. But with Gwinnett's Gateway exam, I could not, in good conscience, look the other way. Schools should be first and foremost a safe haven, where children feel secure, not a place where they are needlessly stressed and made to feel afraid. I'd do it all the same way again if given the chance. Even though I have been threatened with prison, termination, and permanent revocation of my teaching license in a desperate attempt to shut me up, my freedom to speak the truth will not be denied.

In December of 2002 a Superior Court judge in Atlanta cleared James Hope of any wrongdoing in posting the test items and declared that the Professional Standards Commission had insufficient evidence to suspend Hope's teaching license. The PSC will meet in January 2003 to decide whether to accept or appeal the ruling. James Hope can be contacted through e-mail at wildyears3@aol.com.

6

Finding Our Voices

NADINE CORDOVA

SISTERS NADINE AND PATSY CORDOVA, BOTH LONGTIME TEACHERS AT Vaughn High School, in the tiny New Mexico town where they were born, were in Patsy's classroom one afternoon in February of 1997 when they had an unexpected visit from their town's chief of police. The chief, serving as a messenger from school superintendent Arthur Martinez, handed each a letter announcing her suspension from teaching. Their alleged offense? The Cordovas were charged with "insubordination for refusing to teach the prescribed curriculum."

*W*ith the exception of one excellent business teacher, public education taught me only to read the words but never to read the world. School ignored my cultural identity and left me with the sense that something was missing in our lives. With no clear sense of myself reflected in textbooks and incorporated into school rituals and practices, it was impossible for me to find my voice. These painful chapters in my life took twenty-five years to overcome.

In contrast to my experience in schools, my father made me proud to be Mexican. He was uneducated but clearly aware of what I might have to endure in my life. Almost daily, it seemed, he would tell me, "You are a Mexican, never forget your language." Even if it was just a trip to the neighborhood grocery store, I could not leave until I recited my list in Spanish. That used to make me so angry. Why would I need to know the Spanish language? I used to ask myself. My father did not leave a life insurance policy or any kind of inheritance when he died in 1972, but he left me a gift that was worth more than money. He planted the seed that made me appreciate what it meant to be Mexican. The public school system would never fill that void for me. The public schools stripped that pride that my father had instilled in me and made me "American." I was taught in a very subtle, institutionalized manner that there is something shameful in being Mexican.

My sister Patsy still has vivid memories of being threatened with suspension at the age of ten for speaking Spanish on the playground. She grew up ashamed of the food she ate, the accent she spoke with, and the lifestyle that we knew. We never saw ourselves in books. At one point my father worked in the fields in Clovis, New Mexico, about 120 miles from Vaughn, where we grew up. On Sunday evening he would prepare his bedroll, and we would walk him up to the railroad tracks where he would jump in an empty boxcar that would take him to Clovis. On Friday we would wait for him to jump out of the boxcar that would bring him back home.

Yet in the classroom, every story consisted of families that were not brown-skinned. In these stories, there was always a mom and a dad and two children, one boy and one girl, who lived in a cute little house with a white picket fence. The children's pets always had names like Spot. Our dogs were named *Musico* and *Oso*. In these stories, the blond dad in his business suit and tie would pick up his briefcase, get in his car, and go to work. The shame in who we were and how we lived started at a very young age.

Even graduating at the top of my class did not make my choices and direction in life any easier. At the age of twenty-three, I found myself in a situation I could never have predicted. I was a single parent, without a college education, living with my mother and sister, and working minimum wage. This predicament took an enormous toll on my self-esteem. My sister encouraged me to go back to complete my college education and become a teacher. The thought of returning to a university with a small child frightened me, but I decided to take on the challenge in 1982, when my son was two years old. My quest for a better life began with my enrollment at Eastern New Mexico University (ENMU) in Portales, New Mexico.

It was at ENMU that I discovered—purely by chance—that it was pretty cool to be a Mexican. Truthfully, I would never have known that there was such a course as Chicano Humanities if a friend had not recommended it. It came as a complete shock that there were books with my history in it. This course empowered me and gave me strength to endure whatever would happen in my life. Chicano Humanities was the first college text that I read from cover to cover ... the first book that I saw myself in. This is when I found my voice. If this class could change my life, then I was determined that I possessed the knowledge to empower my students.

The combination of discovering my identity and becoming a teacher formed my philosophy in education. Besides my Chicano Humanities professor, there was a special education professor who used to tell us, "If you are not teaching relevant education, then you are not teaching." When I returned to Vaughn to give back to my community, I knew in my heart that I could never be a traditional educator. I would never do to my students what had been done to me. It was then I knew that education was much more than what is found in textbooks. It is about teaching tolerance and respect for people's heritage. If you do not know where you came from, than how can you possibly know where you are going?

In January of 1987 I accepted my first teaching job in my hometown. It was time to make a difference. My sister was already teaching in Vaughn and I knew I could learn from her. She also shared a similar philosophy. In those days relevant materials were scarce and Internet access was foreign to me. I found myself teaching information right out of my Chicano college textbook. My students were totally engaged in this type of curriculum.

Professional staff development consisted of two-hour meetings discussing the renovation of the football field crow's nest, the amount of gravel we needed for the parking lot, and ways to control gum chewing. Could a gum-sniffing dog have solved this problem? There was never a discussion of the educational needs of students.

As educators we didn't have the basics to work with, much less culturally relevant materials, but I did my best to provide new perspectives. Once an Anglo parent came to me, very angry. She was upset that I taught the darker side of Columbus in my class. She said, "How dare you teach my son that Columbus is not a hero." My response was that I was teaching a different perspective, and her son was free to make his own decision about who his heroes were. This was an omen of what was to happen in my future.

Two events became the foundation for my future as a teacher in the Vaughn public schools. The first was the PBS special *Chicano, History of the Mexican American Civil Rights Movement*. My emotions ran high when I discovered that our history was being told in a video. There was no doubt in my mind that I would use these materials in my class. When this special aired on PBS, I recorded it and immediately integrated it into all my classes. It was crucial that all of my students get a glimpse into their past. Seeing the video was also an emotional experience for my students, reinforcing my belief that if there is some type of emotion tied to learning, students will remember what they have learned. One of my seventh-grade students commented, "I can't believe my history has been hidden from me my whole life."

The second event was an article that came out in the *Albuquerque Journal* in May of 1995, about a MEChA organization at another high school. MEChA, which stands for Movimiento Estudiantil Chicanos de Aztlan, gives students the opportunity to learn about their heritage and perform community service. The article caught my attention because it highlighted MEChA's mission to raise the self-esteem of "Hispanic" students by empowering them and helping them discover their identity. Within a couple of days I shared the article with my students and contacted the MEChA sponsor to learn how we could start one of these groups in Vaughn.

By the time the school year began in the fall of 1996, there were twenty-three MEChA members, although our school had only sixty-five students in grades seven through twelve. Our MEChA members were from different cultural backgrounds with a wide range of academic and grade levels. One thing that they had in common was an overwhelming desire to learn about their history and to find their voices. Our MEChA group began making their plans for the upcoming year. They were going to read to the young, visit the elderly, clean the cemetery, put up *luminarias* at Christmas, and last but not least, learn about their Chicano heritage.

Our downfall began with the formation of the MEChA club. On the first day of the school year there was a back-to-school assembly, which everybody in town attends. MEChA members, who had been attending leadership conferences, were so excited about their new group that they wanted to encourage more students to become involved. The two cochairs asked if they could do a presentation at this assembly, and I thought this was a great idea. A group of about five went before the assembly to talk about the club they were starting and about all the fantastic plans they had for the coming year. On their way back to their seats, one of my students felt an overwhelming sense of pride. She then let out the cry that tore the community apart: "Que Viva la Raza, Que Viva el Chicano." You could have heard a pin drop in that gymnasium. We were about to discover the cause of the silence.

That was when the vicious attack started on me. There were accusations that I started a racist and anti-American group. These accusations came from the chairman of the school board, whom we had known all our lives. He claimed that I was building up the self-esteem of Hispanics by tearing down the white race. The accusations were outrageous, unfounded, and unconstitutional. The superintendent informed me in writing that we would not be allowed to announce upcoming MEChA meetings on the intercom, we could not post flyers about MEChA in the hallway, our students were not allowed to speak about MEChA during passing period, and no school resources could be accessed by our group. At that point I knew I had to seek legal counsel.

The American Civil Liberties Union of New Mexico accepted my case within days of receiving my letter, which outlined the discrimination we were facing. The federal lawsuit charged Vaughn school officials with breaching my First Amendment rights. The suit enraged the administration and the school board. During the discovery process, our attorneys began depositions to get at the basis of the accusations and the identities of the people involved. We learned that that the richest "Spanish" man in town was offended by the Chicano perspective of how the Spanish came and killed Native Americans and stole their land. In his deposition, he said the correct perspective was that the Spanish came and "saw a vast amount of unoccupied land and chose to live there." This influential man then told the school board president, "You either fire these women [my sister and me] or I will pull my kids out of the school." The school board president, who is married to a "Spanish" woman, was also offended by MEChA and Chicano history.

As the case progressed, we discovered the depth of the identity issue within our own people. The history of the Mexican American or Chicano is complex, because we have long been known to be a mixed-race people. The instigators of our firing in Vaughn associate their identity with that of the Spanish conquistadors who arrived in New Mexico in the 1600s. New Mexico Spaniards claimed to have endured four hundred–plus years of solitary confinement where no other non-Spaniard had mixed bloodlines with them. We threatened their beliefs by teaching the truth that New Mexicans are mestizos who have blood from the Spaniards, the Native Americans, and the slaves brought from Africa. During the course of the Chicano existence, our blood has spanned many cultures, from Peru to the present-day Southwest.

Without any investigations or proof of wrongdoing, the school board president and the superintendent began a smear campaign that they would live to regret. There was no way I would allow myself to go down without a battle. They were violating my constitutional rights and my academic freedom. After all, by now I had a strong sense of identity and voice.

I continued to teach integrated language arts that included Chicano history and to sponsor MEChA. In order to document the illegal behavior of school officials, I requested that all communication from the administration be in writing. I also insisted that one meeting with the superintendent be tape recorded. I knew that I would need evidence to fight the classist and racist oppression. The letters of attack and tape-recorded meeting would later serve as evidence in a civil rights lawsuit. Even though the attack was mainly focused on me, my sister would also come under attack.

By December, I had received numerous letters stating that I would lose my job if I continued teaching "Chicano" history, although I could teach about other cultures such as African, Native American, and Jewish. According to the superintendent and the chairman of the school board, our history was racist and would offend white people. We were forbidden to use all the Chicano-oriented materials purchased by the school district at the beginning of the school year. The history of my people was being censored.

During the Christmas break, school board representatives searched our rooms. Do you suppose they were looking for our plan to take over the Southwest? They discovered a test review for my language arts class that asked my students to be able to write about terms such as the Constitution of the United States, justice, vision, Robert F. Kennedy, Dolores Huerta, tolerance, Cesar Chavez, and so on. The superintendent took this from my desk and wrote at the top of the test review "to be eliminated from further study." This supposedly educated administrator censored the U.S. Constitution. The school board president also videotaped our classrooms, which would become evidence in our firing.

When the *Albuquerque Journal* learned that Chicano history had been censored in Vaughn and that MEChA was under attack, a reporter contacted me and asked if I would share my story in mid-February. There were no policies that prohibited faculty members from talking to the press and I was well aware that this was my constitutional right. Our story made headline news on the front page of the *Journal*. The interview enraged the administration, and we were told we would be fired, in violation of the school board's own policies, due process, and the Constitution.

Meanwhile, I struggled to maintain a degree of normalcy in my classroom. Since I was accused of teaching racism, I assumed that Teaching Tolerance, an excellent curriculum developed by the Southern Poverty Law Center, would be acceptable, so I began using it. The school administration responded by claiming that we were insubordinate, and on February 28, 1997, my sister and I were both suspended. According to the administration we replaced one racist curriculum with another. I will never forget the day that the Vaughn chief of police brought in our letters of suspension and guarded the classroom door while he waited for our keys.

During the discovery period following our suspension, we learned that the administration could not tell my sister and me apart. They had absolutely no clue who taught what, when we taught the alleged racist curriculum, or which students were actually in our classes.

For the next two years, my sister and I lived quite an exciting life. Organizations from coast to coast invited us to tell our story at their conferences. We had to be fired to see the Statue of Liberty. Some of the places where we spoke were Amherst, Tufts University, and Washington State. We also spoke at universities in Sacramento, San Diego, San Luis Obispo, San Francisco, Tucson, and Greensville, South Carolina. Among our other speaking engagements were conferences in St. Louis, Grand, Junctio, Boulder, Orlando, and many New Mexico locations. We were thrilled to meet so many great people who understood and recognized our struggle.

In July of 1997, the Vaughn school board scheduled a hearing at which we would be able to present our case and the board would decide our future. Apparently, the mayor and his good old boys expected a scene out of a Mexican Mafia movie, because they contacted the National Guard and requested their attendance at the firing of the Cordova sisters when they heard that many of our supporters would be at the hearing. The mayor was full of pride that he protected his city from outsiders, as he explained it to our attorneys. Many dangerous university professors and students from all over New Mexico showed up to demonstrate their support. As expected, we were fired within the first ten minutes.

As our lawsuit proceeded, the school district attorneys deposed my sister and me. We then discovered some of the evidence they had on us. When Patsy was being deposed, the attorney asked the secretary to bring in the TV and VCR. We were about to discover what was on the video they had recorded in our classrooms. The accusations were that we had racist posters that taught militancy with fists raised in the air and encouraged disrespect for the white race. The attorney popped in the videotape and there were our classrooms. He showed my sister a beautiful poster from *Chicano, History of the Civil Rights Movement,* with images of successful Mexican Americans. At the bottom there was a black silhouette, which the attorney asked my sister to explain. Patsy said, "Those are graduates, holding their diplomas."

The attorney said, *"What?"* and pushed the zoom button. The graduates holding their diplomas came zooming in much larger than they had first appeared. The attorney said, "Oh!" and turned off the TV. The videotape was never mentioned again.

During this same deposition, the attorney brought out the book *500 Years of Chicano History,* which had been purchased by the school. He asked my sister questions along this line:

QUESTION: "Where did you get this book?"
ANSWER: "From the Southwest Organizing Project in Albuquerque."
QUESTION: "Who was responsible for ordering this book?"
ANSWER: "I think it was Nadine. She got together with Lorenzo Garcia from Albuquerque. He was organizing a drug prevention through cultural awareness program in Vaughn."
QUESTION: "Were you at the meeting?'
ANSWER: "No."
QUESTION: "Who else was at this meeting?"

By this time the attorney was almost whispering, as if the meeting were too covert to discuss aloud. My sister was tempted to whisper, "Fidel Castro was at the meeting."

These examples are intended to show how outrageous people can get when they are attempting to take your voice by censoring your history. They were not successful because in November 1998, we reached an out-of-court settlement of our lawsuit against the school district. In addition to a substantial cash payment and removal of negative letters placed in our personnel files, the settlement also included a reinstatement of our teaching positions, but by then we had already moved on with our lives. Subsequently, we went on to win awards such as ACLU's Guardian of the Constitution, Archdiocese of Santa Fe's Pilgrimage for Peace, Defense of Academic Freedom from the National Council of Social Studies, the Civil Rights Award from the city of Albuquerque, and Multi-Cultural Educator of the Year from the National Association of Multi-Cultural Education. Most recently we received a letter from the National Council of Teachers of English that we will be presented with an Intellectual Freedom Award in October.

Although we have received many awards and were able to travel throughout the country telling our story, we also lost our jobs and had to leave our homes. My sister left her home, where she took care of our aging mother, who is suffering from Alzheimer's disease, and moved to Albuquerque. My mother is now in a nursing home. I pulled my children from the Vaughn schools and also moved to Albuquerque. My husband and my home remained in Vaughn. For five years, I have commuted over two hundred miles every weekend so that my son can spend time with his father. This is the most painful consequence of what happened to us.

We can no longer help our students in Vaughn discover their voices, but if we can help other teachers see that possibilities are only limited by their minds and hearts, what happened to us is worth it. We are not recommending that teachers get fired so they can file lawsuits, travel, and get awards. By telling our story we are trying to show that in the end justice prevails for the benefit of our students. There is a large support system out there to encourage teachers to do the right thing. Although there is a danger that teachers who speak out will be considered a threat to the school system and will lose their jobs, we cannot teach in fear. The curriculum I constructed and defended was based strictly on my personal experience, but today there is considerable research to support these much-needed changes in our classrooms. We have to follow our values and remain strong for the sake of our children. Until they are able to discover their voice, we are their voice.

All educators should reflect on what and how we teach. What is the real purpose of "education?" Is it to continue the status quo? Is it to score above the fiftieth percentile on the Terra Nova test? Or is to empower students, help them understand their world and become intelligent future leaders with a strong sense of self? Obviously, the system is failing miserably at attaining the scores, so why not work at building critical thinkers? Why not take the risk and teach tolerance? Let's go beyond tolerance and teach our youth to respect and value each other.

A high school MEChA member whom we had the honor of meeting at a conference summed up our experience quite wisely. This young man, who might have been fifteen, stated quite proudly, "Right on, Cordovas, you did the right thing. They can take your job, but they cannot take your heart."

After being fired by the Vaughn school board, Nadine Cordova was unemployed for a year before returning to work as an administrative assistant in the University of New Mexico chicano studies department. From 2000–2002 she taught at two schools in Albuquerque. In the fall of 2002 she and her sister Patsy both began teaching at Washington Middle School in Albuquerque.

7

There and Back Again

PEGGIE BORING

PEGGIE BORING LIKES TO QUOTE ALBERT EINSTEIN WHEN DISCUSSING HER teaching philosophy: "It is the supreme art of the teacher to awaken joy in creative expression and knowledge." Even as she demonstrated supreme art as a drama teacher in Black Mountain, North Carolina, she was transferred from the school where she had been so successful. Although the play she and her students had chosen for state competition, *Independence*, had been approved by the administration and won awards at regional competition, it was labeled "obscene" by the principal. Her career marred by the accusation, Peggie Boring was forced to fight for the right to "awaken joy in creative expression" and for her students' rights to engage in such joy.

The summer before school opened in 1991 was the best of times. The school system had built a brand-new Charles D. Owen High School campus, moving from Swannanoa, North Carolina, to Black Mountain, North Carolina. Chris Slay, the technical director for The Valley Community Theatre (our community/school partnership) and I had designed a state-of-the-art theatre space for this new school. The theatre had a real fly system, orchestra pit, scene shop, dressing rooms, sound and lighting systems, headsets, and an intercom system enabling the stage manager to communicate with the set crew, lighting crew, and those in the dressing rooms. The acoustics were perfect.

Our theatre group needed and deserved such a space. We were, after all, an extraordinary troupe, second to none, graduating students to Cornell, Yale, Webster, Southern Methodist, DePaul, Otterbein, Hofstra, New York University, and North Carolina School of the Arts, to mention a few. Our theatre students were second only to students in the athletic program in total scholarship money awarded to seniors. Individual students won a variety of prestigious theatre awards, and our theatre won regional and state awards for acting, ensemble work, set, lighting, costuming, makeup, directing, and literary adaptation. We were the North Carolina Honor Troupe. I was honored with the North Carolina Robroy Farquhar Award for contributions to secondary school theatre and the C. C. Lipscomb Award for Best Director, North Carolina. We won performance awards at the state Thespian conference and were selected to perform at the International Thespian Festival. We were also an award-winning competitive acting team. We showed others that "Redneck Tech" in "Swannanowhere" *was* somewhere!

My fourteenth year guiding these young people was going to be amazing—great students in a great facility. My new, inexperienced students were excited about "learning the ropes." They were assigned technical crews and began their acting classes. I found two vehicles for my advanced students. Both were bold, interesting, and requiring great stretching and skill. Neither story line was a "teenage pity piece" involving teen pregnancy, teen substance abuse, or teen relationships. Both plays included characters of all ages, requiring the actors to move outside their comfortable frame of reference in order to explore the complexities of choices and consequences.

The choice for my four most advanced actresses was Lee Blessing's *Independence*. The play explores the relationships in an intensely and severely dysfunctional family—a divorced, emotionally disturbed mother and her three daughters, each of whom has emotional problems of her own. One of the daughters is a lesbian, another is pregnant with an illegitimate child, and the third is a rebellious young woman whose colorful vocabulary includes the four-letter F word. Is this heavy stuff? Yes. Is that what the play is about? No. Does the play condone their actions? No. The play is about love, compassion, communication, and forgiveness—family values all. It was to be one of our entries to the North Carolina Theatre Conference One-Act Play Festival.

I had four remarkable advanced actresses—two seniors, who were eighteen, and one junior, who was seventeen and turned eighteen during the production. They were mature, responsible, intelligent, and seasoned. The three seniors had actively participated in our program for three years, the junior for two. We traveled all over North Carolina and to the International Thespian

Festival in order for them to see all different types of theatre from around the world. I roomed with them, shared their meals, and listened to their problems, not only as their teacher but also as their friend. The young woman who played the mother was an asthmatic and I always held a power of attorney in case of a medical emergency. I taught her older sister, who went on to Yale and Chapel Hill. Another of the four students brought her dog and stayed with me while her mother was in the hospital. As a part of their growing-up years, I knew them as well as I knew my own children. I had absolutely no doubt they were ready for this acting challenge.

I sent copies of the scripts home, asking the girls to discuss the play with their parents to make certain they were all comfortable with the subject matter and language. The parents certainly took note of the power, passion, depth, and strength of the script. They also noticed the language—but the families were completely supportive. The consensus was that the script provided compelling lessons in our common humanity and material their daughters could handle philosophically and dramatically. We all felt that such a powerful piece, requiring superlative acting skills, would bring recognition not only from adjudicators, but also present possibilities for scholarships and exposure to college instructors and their programs. As Drew Lindsay reported in the article "Dramatic License" in *Education Week*, "The competition was a chance for the kids from Owen, a little school bunkered in the Swannanoa Valley, to square off against the big-city kids from Raleigh and Charlotte. It was also an opportunity for them to catch the eye of college drama instructors, win scholarships, and get a ticket out of the place some of them called 'Swannanowhere.'" The accolades would be in the form of credentials for their resumes. The material would ensure excellent performance pieces for college auditions. College recruiters would see them perform. One of their mothers remarked, "We knew this wasn't a play we could invite Aunt Bessie to, but it was for a competition, and we understood that. It was our daughters' chance to get scholarships and go off to college." Her daughter, who won a Best Actress award, portrayed the lesbian, Kess, and went on to receive full financial aid at Webster University in St. Louis, Missouri. They also knew the play was not for viewing at large. It was a competition piece that would be judged solely on its artistic merit. It would stand or fall on the capabilities of these four actresses and their ability to convey the author's message. Knowing the ability and maturity of these four actresses, I was confident that we could avoid the wrathful, scathing critiques I've seen judges visit on directors who choose plays that aren't suitable for their students.

As I did every year, I informed the principal of the title and author of the plays we were doing that year. I didn't provide any specific details of any of the plays because he never attended any of our performances, did not indicate any evidence of support for any portion of our program, and I had no reason to believe the reception would be any different that year. I didn't think he read the selections submitted to him from the English department's reading list either. Rehearsals for this particular play were closed to other students but were always open to parents and administration. In fact, under a former principal, a student and I had collaborated on a play, *Ep'-i-logue,* that contained mature subject matter. The principal attended a rehearsal and simply asked if the play was to be produced for the school. Since it, too, was a competition piece, the answer was no. He wished us well and it never became an issue. That play advanced to state finals and was selected to be produced at the International Thespian Festival.

At regional competition, *Independence* won every single award except Best Actor: the actress portraying Kess won Best Actress; the actresses portraying the other daughters won Honorable Mentions for Acting; and the entire cast was presented with the award for Ensemble Acting. Our other entry won similar awards. Both advanced to the state finals, winning the two allotted slots for our region.

Before the state competition, two members of the *Independence* cast told their English class, which was complaining about the problematic Shakespearean text they were reading, that plays are best appreciated in performance and that issues pertinent to Shakespeare's time are relevant today. Their teacher suggested that the *Independence* cast might perform the play for her English class. I agreed, providing certain conditions were met. Though the two cast members had recounted the elements of the play to her, I cautioned her about the mature subject matter and language and urged her to get approval from the administration and require permission slips. Apprised of the content of the play, students could elect not to see the play. Following the performance, I led a discussion of the issues involved, the language, and the audience reaction, as I answered questions.

Although theatre productions were not included in the school district's controversial materials policy at that time, I followed the requirements set forth in the policy for literature.

At this point, I believed John Locke: "The only fence against the world is a thorough knowledge of it." I also agreed with Learned Hand in his speech to the Board of Regents of the State University of New York: "The mutual confidence on which all else depends can be maintained only by an open mind and a brave reliance upon free discussion." Unfortunately, I was a member of a small minority. A parent complained to the principal and my journey began.

"I wish it need not have happened in my time," said Frodo.

"So do I," said Gandalf, "and so do all who live to see such times, but that is not for them to decide. All we have to decide is what to do with the time that is given us."

"I am not made for perilous quests," cried Frodo. "Why did it come to me? Why was I chosen?"

"Such questions cannot be answered," said Gandalf. "You may be sure that it was not for any merit that others do not possess: not for power or wisdom at any rate. But you have been chosen, and you must use such strength and heart and wits as you have."

—J.R.R. Tolkien, *The Lord of the Rings: The Fellowship of the Ring*

Following the parent's complaint, the principal asked for a copy of the script, then decreed that we would not be permitted to perform *Independence* at state competition. I invited him and the superintendent of schools to see a performance along with the parents of the cast. They declined. The actresses' parents urged the principal to allow the show to be performed for state competition. He agreed, provided we make some cuts. We won alternate winner at the state competition and I understood another truth: "Fear of serious injury cannot alone justify suppression of free speech and assembly. Men feared witches and burned women. It is the function of speech to free men from the bondage of irrational fears" (Honorable Louis Brandeis, *Whitney v. California*).

On June 2, 1992, my teacher evaluation ratings were "superior" and "well above standard" in all function areas. Ten days later, my principal requested that I be transferred from the school, citing "personal conflicts resulting from actions initiated during the course of the school year." I learned of my transfer from a copy of a memorandum sent to the personnel office.

The superintendent claimed that I had failed to comply with the school system's controversial materials policy, which suddenly included drama, even though I had followed the guidelines set forth for literature. I was reassigned to teach theatre at the middle school level.

I appealed the decision to the board of education. The weeks leading up to the board hearing were terrible times. The dark forces of Mordor were gathering. There were accusations, reported in the newspapers and television, that the play was obscene and that I was immoral. Teachers I had known for fourteen years were afraid to be around me for fear of retaliation. At a support gathering, I saw several teachers sitting for a long time in a car outside the building. Finally, they drove off. I can only assume they thought better of coming in. A banner was spread across a storefront in Black Mountain congratulating the principal on his protection of community values. At a breakfast honoring him and the school's Christian athletes, he was again lauded for his stand.

At the hearing on September 2, 1992, the school board upheld my transfer. In an instant, the community where I had taught for fourteen years was polarized. Under the headline "Friends and Supporters of Owen High School," a six-by-nine-inch print advertisement appeared: "We the undersigned

ministers and Christian lay persons of the Swannanoa Valley approve and
endorse the action regarding the transfer of Peggie Boring from Owen High
School's Drama Department." They went on to declare their appreciation for
the school officials' "commitment to academic excellence and sensitivity to
community values." They registered their "moral outrage toward the presentation of the play, *Independence*, to students at Owen High School . . . the play
contained profanity (four-letter words), took God's name in vain, blasphemed
the name of Jesus, presented sexual promiscuity, premarital sex, adultery, and
homosexuality." The advertisement was signed by fifty-two individuals, including twelve Baptist ministers, one Methodist and one Presbyterian min-
ister, the mayor of Black Mountain (who was on the school board), and one
person who identified herself as a lifetime member of the Thespian Society. I
remember reading it and thinking that I had taught for fourteen years in that
community. They knew me. And they knew me better than that. Ironically,
the principal approved the showing of *Wayne's World* to student body members who had sold enough wrapping paper in that year's school fund-raiser.
I, on the other hand, felt as if I had been shoved out the front door to stand
alone. Metaphorically, as well as physically, Owen High sits on a hill, and that
entrance looms over its surroundings.

Orcs crawled out of their dark places to throw stones. I received hate
mail. Several quoted their ministers' admonitions to "hate the sin, but love the
sinner," but admitted having to pray about hating me. The program I had
worked fourteen years to develop was dismantled in front of me. Plaques and
awards were given randomly to students. Because of the community polariza-
tion and deteriorating direction, the community theatre I helped found eight
years ago disintegrated. I was in the newspaper and on television. One morning, on my way to my car, I looked down at the newspaper. It was rolled up, held
together by a rubber band across my face. In my imagination I saw that image
being repeated in every front yard in Buncombe County. I was constantly on
the nightly news, which reported every meeting, positive or negative, discussed
every nuance of every comment made, and showed the same unflattering file
footage of me leaving the school board meeting, after the upholding of my
transfer. In a public meeting, a local newspaper editor looked directly at me
and said with disdain, "I never met anyone in the limelight who didn't want
to be there." My grandson, in the first grade at the time, asked me, "Grandma,
why do they hate you?"

I added another lesson: "It is easier to perceive error than to find truth,
for the former lies on the surface and is easily seen, while the latter lies in the
depth, where few are willing to search for it." Goethe's words spoke directly to
my heart. During that time, my perceived errors were certainly discussed and
debated. My imperfections never seemed more visible and I have never been

so painfully vulnerable. But I believe there is truth that lies in the depth for those who are willing to see it.

And, like Frodo, I did have my own Fellowship. Dirck Cruser, one of the kindest, gentlest and strongest men I have ever met, formed a band of stalwart souls to stand by my side. He called his band GRO—Get it Right at Owen. The American Civil Liberties Union; Luke Largess, of the law firm of Fergusson, Stein, and Wallace; Monroe Gilmour, an outspoken and principled social activist in Black Mountain; students, parents, and teachers rallied to protest. For every ugly, self-righteous letter to the editor that appeared, they, professors from college and university programs with whom I had worked, and directors of community theatres wrote letters of support. I can't imagine what I would have done without these brave friends. Dirck, Monroe, and my family literally held my hand, put their arms around my shoulders, and made me strong when I was not. My former father-in-law marched up to a school board member and made him admit I had been "railroaded."

My name became "Plaintiff," as in "Plaintiff alleges that prior to the hearing there was considerable public discussion of the transfer, including that the play was obscene and that she was immoral. She alleges that members of the school board asked questions at the hearing that demonstrated their consideration of matters outside the evidence presented at the hearing." I filed a lawsuit in federal court on January 10, 1994. My amended complaint claimed that my transfer was in retaliation for expression of unpopular views through the production of the play and thus in violation of my right to freedom of speech under the First and Fourteenth Amendments and Article I, Section 14 of the North Carolina Constitution. I also claimed a violation of due process under the Fourteenth Amendment and Article I, Section 19 of the North Carolina Constitution based on the allegation that members of the school board considered information that was not presented at the hearing; and a violation of a liberty interest under Article I, Sections 1 and 19 of the North Carolina Constitution. The defendants were the members of the Buncombe County School Board, individually, and as a group, the superintendent and the principal of Charles D. Owen High School. The district court decided against "Plaintiff" on each of these claims. I appealed only the dismissal of my federal First Amendment claim.

I was transferred to Valley Springs Middle School, Arden, North Carolina. "Hello, I'm Peggie Boring and I'll bet you're glad you're not." That's how I felt and how I introduced myself during the first faculty meeting of the year, when the new teachers were asked to stand and tell a little about themselves. Their faces wore expressions of naked curiosity: Who is this woman? How did she arrive at this moment in time? Why did she do it? How has this situation affected her? My colleagues laughed, their faces relaxed. And, yes, Valley Springs was good to me. The faculty, administration, parents, and students helped the healing process. They supported me, helped me regain my confidence and self-esteem, and provided me with a safe refuge while I regrouped and the forces around me raged. My principal, Arbie Rhodes, told me to hold my head up and wear lots of red lipstick. I did hate being the constant current event in social studies classes and I did encounter the occasional child who told me her friend's mother told her I was fired from high school for doing "dirty plays." But the principals there were confident of my play selections and when a parent felt the need to question my choice of *Joseph and the Amazing Technicolor Dreamcoat*, the administration took my side. And that's what it's all about.

One day, I went to see a personal banker at my local bank. "I am Peggie Boring," I told him. "I know who you are," he smirked. That was the last straw; for the fact of the matter was, he *did not* know me. He "knew" the one-dimensional, cardboard cut-out, file footage Peggie Boring who did dirty plays with young students. Unable to speak for the large lump in my throat and with a plastic smile on my face, I turned on my heel and left. No more media, no more letters, no more hate, no more awkward moments when the superintendent and I met at school functions, no more tears, no more depression, no more fear. It was time to leave the carnage behind.

I visited a magnet school for the performing and visual arts in Charlotte, North Carolina, a part of the Charlotte-Mecklenburg school system. Before long, I was hired to teach English from February to June, and then I was to pick up theatre classes the following school year. I sold my home and left Asheville quietly, leaving behind my oldest son and his family. The media didn't know I had relocated. The following school year I became department chair for theatre. Ironically, I served on the media selection committee, reviewing controversial books and plays. My life settled into a deeply satisfying pattern of teaching and directing.

The American Civil Liberties Union honored me with the Person of the Year Award for defending the First Amendment, and I received the Dr. Marketta Laurella Free Speech Award. I spoke to various conventions and groups, including the Educational Theatre Association at their annual convention in San Diego, California. I was introduced by Jim Palmarini, a representative from the Educational Theatre Association who had seen *Independence*. He repeated a remark made by the actress who portrayed Kess. After meeting her following the performance, he asked her what her experience in *Independence* had meant to her. She replied, "It made me a better person." I have never felt so humble in my life. That remark made everything I had ever accomplished, or ever will accomplish, worthwhile. That said to me that Peggie Boring had grown up to be a real teacher.

Meanwhile, the case was crawling up the judicial ladder, headed for the United States Supreme Court. Was this simply an employee/employer dispute? Had I been deprived of my First Amendment rights? Was I overstepping my teaching responsibilities by attempting to control the curriculum or flouting the controversial materials policy? The issues were debated, appealed, and counterappealed. The votes were always very close. I lost the case on the district level, to win 2–1 on appeal in the first encounter with the Fourth Circuit Court of Appeals. The lawyers for the other side appealed and requested an *en banc* hearing—a hearing by the full fifteen-judge panel. I lost that appeal 8–7. Eventually, the case reached the United States Supreme Court and the Charlotte-Mecklenburg school system realized whom they had working for them.

The media found me, too. I can only imagine their chagrin and confusion when they realized I didn't live in Asheville any longer, and they couldn't find a phone number or address for me, because I didn't live in Charlotte, but forty-five miles away in Lincolnton, North Carolina. Of course, they tracked me through the school system and began to call and visit the school. I left word at the front office that I was not to be called out of class, nor were visitors allowed to visit during class without my prior approval. The students, and many teachers, were thunderstruck when my identity surfaced. The students loved the attention and, being theatre people, fought over being in photographs. They were funny, protective, and supportive.

Then, one day three years later, while I was teaching class, a local journalist came to the theatre. There was sadness and compassion in his face—and I knew. He took me aside, wanting to tell me before I could be taken by surprise, giving me time to compose my face and prepare my words. The Supreme Court had declined to hear my case, remanding it to the Fourth Circuit Court of Appeals. Teachers are not covered by First Amendment rights. My statement was the same that I had given to the Asheville *Citizen-Times* years ago. Sometimes the winning is in the fight.

Why did I pursue this arduous course? It wasn't premeditated. I didn't think to myself, "It's time to shake up the establishment. How far can I push the envelope?" As the furor escalated, the fundamental certainty that emerged for me was: This is not just. It is not equitable. I had always given everything I had: 100 percent, the best of my ability. I had always tried to do the right thing. I wanted four remarkable actresses to reach their potential, to put those higher-level thinking skills into practice, to find joy in creative expression and knowledge. It is not right that for my efforts, those whom I trusted to be my advocates were afraid to admit the existence of contrary opinions, or to suspend their own; instead they chose to replace an open mind and free discussions with the special interests of a particular group. I felt helpless and betrayed.

I wish more than anything that I could end my journey as Bilbo Baggins wanted to end his: "And they lived happily ever after." That was not to be. I suffered a bitter and painful separation from the magnet school. I took early retirement. And, yes, I think my past was ultimately used as an unspoken threat until I succumbed. My delight is serving as state director for the Educational Theatre Association and International Thespian Society. I don't have a high school troupe, but I can still reach youth through my work with them. Teaching still defines my life.

This is who I am and how I arrived at this moment. Is there a lesson I can leave? I have been asked repeatedly to give advice to all performing and visual arts educators, as well as community theatre groups. Here are my thoughts. Be afraid. Be very afraid. I did my best. I thought I was doing the right things. It seems that teachers and all members of the arts family walk the razor's edge. I have never met one educator whose objective is to shock, corrupt anyone's morals, or present material for its prurient interest to audiences young *or* old. Funds to arts groups are tied by strings to subjective views of subject matter or are withdrawn altogether. I don't think most people willingly raise Stepford children, too fragile to perceive the agony and the ecstasy of humanity.

My advice is never to give up. Try not to give in to the temptation to wash your hands of conflict, to hide, or to resign, no matter how unpleasant the situation. There is a Fellowship for your support, too.

Join reputable, legitimate organizations and lobby for change. Aid them in advancing the cause of educating the public. Document successes and statistics. Students in the arts really do make better SAT and ACT scores. Publicize and recognize awards and scholarships in the arts; those students represent their school, too, and their accomplishments should make the school and community proud.

Encourage the arts community to work together to enlighten citizens. At the end of another of Lee Blessing's plays, *Eleemosynary*, Echo says, "(I am) someone who loves you, someone who can make you love me. Nearly all the time. I'm going to stay with you. I'm going to prepare you for me. I'm going to cultivate you. I'm going to *tend* you." Her mother, Artie, replies, "Do you think I'm a garden?" Echo responds, "Yes. And you need work." Give the naysayer a new frame of reference. Believe that times of fear and hate will pass. Times will change. Pendulums have a way of swinging in the other direction.

Last, stand up and be counted.

"I wish to make an announcement," he said. He spoke this last word so loudly and suddenly that everyone sat up who still could. "I regret to announce that—though, as I said, eleventy-one years is far too short a time to spend among you—this is the END. I am going. I am leaving NOW. GOOD-BYE!"

There was a blinding flash of light, and the guests all blinked.

Peggie Boring has taught in North Carolina schools for twenty-three years. She is currently an English instructor at Gaston College in Gastonia, North Carolina. She can be reached at pboring@abts.net.

8

Teaching Defiantly: Who Says Bombing Villages Is Patriotic?

IAN HARVEY

PUBLIC SCHOOLS ALL OVER THE COUNTRY RESPONDED TO THE EVENTS OF September 11, 2001, with an outpouring of patriotic symbolism. While some schools offered counseling to traumatized children and created meaningful humanitarian and memorial projects, often the responses took the form of frenzied flag-waving initiated by adults. In one Florida school, children were instructed to "dress like the flag" on Fridays, and in many others pledges and patriotic songs took the place of dialogue and discussion.

In this hyper-patriotic atmosphere, what happens to a high school teacher who actively promotes peace in public demonstrations outside school, presents dissenting viewpoints in the classroom, and challenges the conventional wisdom that all teachers must remain neutral on ethical and moral issues? Ian Harvey, steelworker-turned-teacher, poet, and unapologetic advocate of the underdog, found out the hard way. His story raises important questions about the nature of education and the rights of teachers who challenge prevailing orthodoxies.

---

 ree, Free Palestine!" they chanted into our local antiwar group's megaphone when I proudly offered it to them. On April 20, 2002, in a light D.C. rain, Palestinian mothers, fathers, teenagers, and little kids waved flags of a nation yet to come, wearing their *koufiyyas* in a myriad of ways, in the largest U.S. demonstration since the Eighties. Hasidic rabbis chanted from the podium, "We are all Palestinians! We are all Colombians!"

Weeks later, I was on the Fox network show *The O'Reilly Factor* for a couple of minutes, and although Bill O'Reilly interrupted all of the few sentences of response he allotted me, I had the chance to chuckle on national TV at his heavy-handed censorship and repeat several times that all violence is immoral. Even Ray Parker of the Naples Daily "Noose" wrote a balanced article after the O'Reilly show. Thanks to Michael Moore's website, I still receive a few email messages of support every week (down from a few hundred a week this winter)—messages from all over the world, from parents, students, and teachers who believe that freedom of speech is not negotiable, that even high school students have the right to the truth no matter whom it offends. The tide has turned for me and against the post-September 11 reaction, and the causes of peace and truth will be vindicated in the courts of history and public opinion, vindication of which I was almost sure almost from the start....

Growing up with a cold, dictatorial, businessman father and a sensitive, passive, housewife mother, I was a kid who lived in his imagination, pretending to be a horse first and then later, an Indian. My poor mother had to read *The Story of Ferdinand*, about the pacifist bull, countless times if she expected me to sleep at night.

Looking back as far as I can remember—I guess about the age of five—and ever since—I have always had an affinity for and attraction to the "misfit," the "underdog," and the "lost cause," I suppose because I, too, knew what it was like to be victimized. I saw my mother and sister being victimized as well, by someone more powerful than each of us individually. None of us knew then that we needed each other's solidarity, suffering quietly alone instead. We each sought escape in denial, obsessive behaviors, and imagination. Horses, Native people, and soaring birds must have been emblems for me of that escape. My first occupational goals were to become an ornithologist or a horse veterinarian when I grew up, so I could be as close as possible to the objects of my affection. I think I admired them because they represented the natural grace and palpable freedom I must have craved then—and still do now.

Pain and suffering in Vietnam and the protests against it were on the minds of people in the small town in Pennsylvania where my family moved from Canada in 1966. Most people were concerned solely about the many local young men going off to fight, and we were so far removed from any centers of political discussion that most of what I knew of antiwar sentiment I heard in the song lyrics of bands like Jefferson Airplane and Crosby, Stills, Nash, and Young. No one I knew actually *did* anything to show disagreement with the war. There were no Black people for miles, but racism against them was everywhere. Reading and listening to music were the first ways another world opened up to me, a world in which people did not always do what they were told and did not always believe what they heard from those who had authority over their lives, a world certainly not revealed to me at home or in school for the most part.

Near the end of my high school days of boredom, skipping class, and low grades, working far below my "potential," I read Dee Brown's *Bury My Heart at Wounded Knee* around the same time the American Indian movement occupied that sad location in our sad history. Native people making history right *now* as I watched—heroic people willing to die for their freedom—made me begin to consider activism. But it wasn't until several years later, during the Sandinista revolution, when I was a grad student in Pittsburgh and an FSLN (Frente Sandinista de Liberacion Nacional) member and teacher came to town that I had the chance to act, if only by driving her and her interpreter around to speaking engagements. Estela was an ordinary person, a teacher, making brave sacrifices for her own future and that of her fellow Nicaraguans by fighting as a soldier and joining the literacy campaign after the revolution. She inspired me because I had always been trained to think that most people are powerless to act directly in their own most important interests.

While I was a graduate student in the English department at Pitt, the campus/labor movement against South African apartheid and U.S. aid to Salvadoran death squads and the contras in Nicaragua empowered me to talk about my politics in class as a teaching assistant working with undergrads. I also wrote about my views in relation to the literature we were studying in my own classes as a grad student. Most of my adult life I had gotten the impression that people were either doers or dreamers, and that I belonged exclusively to the latter group. I thought people were born poets like Shelley and Shakespeare supposedly were, never having to rewrite, the greatest poetry in English pouring out of them spontaneously in intricate rhyme schemes. The sainted Gandhi and King could do what no one else could do, I thought, instead of knowing that ordinary people do extraordinary things. It was not until I began to consider teaching as a career that I came to the conclusion—a necessary one for me to *be* a teacher—that a person could be both an activist and a facilitator of the discussion of ideas, a teacher, and that the myth of "objectivity" projected on teachers in a liberal arts educational tradition was only that, a myth. My professors at Pitt were entranced by that grand idea of the disinterested, "déclassé," and I would say, elitist, priest-like role of the teacher and intellectual. No one taught me the words and actions of teachers like Freire, Chomsky, and Zinn.

My grad days at Pitt began a pattern of resistance: to my teaching "superiors," that is, department heads and principals; to the curriculum; and to any abrogation of the tenet that all teachers and all reasonable people must pursue truth. Even though this pursuit will never end, it cannot begin without the founding assumption that *all* ideas we can gather must be addressed. Real classroom discussion requires a leap of faith in itself, because teachers are often afraid of untamed ideas. My own attitude and practice began with the conviction that teachers, especially, must believe passionately in what moral truth is to them as human beings.

However, I learned quickly at Pitt that the way to fit in there was to undermine wittily, as in some highbrow yet trivial word game, every action that could possibly be taken to actualize and defend an idea, to simply deconstruct the idea and the plan for carrying it out, to explain it all away as utopian or dogmatic. We were supposed to see that the gap between theory and practice is too wide to bridge and that in a liberal arts education all ideas are equal anyway. We were supposed to sit around at seminar tables and in classrooms as teachers talking about the advantages and problems of all frameworks for viewing the world. All ideas are problematic, so all we could do as academics was talk. The professors who made this academic function clear to us basked smugly in the privilege bestowed upon them by their position and in this same dogmatic, laissez-faire relativism that kept them in those rooms away from the people in the streets below. I believe that they hoped their students and the students of their students had no ideas they actually wanted to put into action. The same paternalism born of fear rules over high school students here in Florida as well.

During my battles as a grad student trying to discuss, write about, and teach ideas, and to combine activism and theory, I left my ivy-draped tower lair with no money or benefits to work in a steelworker-organized forge shop and write poetry. On a vacation to southwest Florida one November about three years later, when back home the icy wind off the Allegheny River was whipping through the mill, I fell in love with the balmy air and ever-changing, magnificent sky of the Gulf coast. We moved there right away.

Another factory job and then another job cleaning restaurants followed until I began substitute teaching in Pinellas County. I was drawn to the classroom again because I saw it as one place where ideas ought to matter, although my experience had taught me that "official" ones mattered much more. Eventually I joined the English department of Immokalee High School, where I stayed for about seven years and might have never left, because Immokalee, a town of farm workers, was and still is the kind of place where I should teach, even though I spent half of my time at the high school there in a battle against a shouting, megalomaniacal principal, whom I fought to keep my classroom a place for student and teacher creativity and participation in the world as public citizens, expressing our rights and defending the rights of others.

I have known since second grade with Mrs. Frieberg that "education" is nothing close to it. She kept me after school, standing behind me in her attempts to scold and shame me into rolling my whole forearm as I wrote—the "right" way at the time—instead of moving my hand and wrist alone—the "wrong" way—despite the fact that she wasn't dissatisfied with my actual handwriting. I grew a huge corn on my middle finger from gripping my pencil too tightly, and my stomach became so perpetually upset (or maybe I made that up), that I "couldn't go" to school. My parents thought I had an ulcer. Mrs. Frieberg succeeded in teaching me that what we call "education" is really indoctrination designed to teach obedience to power. In contrast, true education is a process of liberating our minds from orthodoxies in order to see the world for ourselves. But the propaganda of the indoctrination system, which conveniently teaches that propaganda only exists in dictatorships we don't support, is so ubiquitous and insidious that students and teachers who attempt to make of education what we think it should be find out quickly and painfully that *we* will be accused of indoctrination and brainwashing. Even believing this for so long did not prepare me for what has happened to me since the winter of 2001.

A handful of us in Naples—elderly, middle-aged, and teenage—decided that we *had* to protest publicly and locally against the bombing of Afghanistan that threatened to starve millions of women and children—besides the ones killed by the bombs themselves. I announced our first protest for December 9, 2001, in a letter to the editor of the *Naples Daily News*, knowing that it would be printed there as had been many of my letters before—pro-immigrant, pro-environment, pro-worker, pro-peace . . . all of them vitriol-provoking in this conservative town.

After my announcement letter was printed, anonymous callers threatened to kill me if we protested in Naples. We were surrounded that first Sunday afternoon by angry men gunning their Harleys and then trying on foot to block our way—unsuccessfully—through the parking lot to the corner of US 41. They said they'd get me fired, and now that I am under investigation by the commissioner of education of Florida, it's clear that some people in Naples are still dedicated to that goal.

In editorials, columns, and letters to the editor, the only local paper, the *Naples Daily News*, owned by media giant Scripps Howard, led the charge against me, quoting me out of context and telling outright lies about what I said or wrote. They persisted in identifying me as a member of the ANSWER (Act Now to Stop War & End Racism) coalition, because my name appeared at its website, although, as I told reporter Ray Parker, there are no members in the sense of a political organization, that ANSWER was and is a loose confederation of many different groups and individuals united in the cause of peace. Writers in the paper alleged that my support of rock-throwing Palestinian youth (which I had once mentioned in a poetry magazine) in the *intifadas* made me a supporter of terrorism, of course avoiding any mention of U.S.-sponsored Israeli state terrorism. There were calls for my lynching in the letters to the editor on a regular basis and misrepresentations of my political views on the front page. The paper also cheered on the district investigation of me, scolding my bosses for the "mild" treatment I was getting from them.

The district investigation of my "teaching practices" began about a week after our first protest because some of the pro-war cheerleaders who had threatened my life had also complained to the central administration that a teacher protesting the bombing of Afghanistan was allowed to continue teaching. The *Naples Daily News* used the example of what it termed a teacher with treasonous and dangerous ideas working in the system to criticize the local teachers' union as "too powerful," although the union did little to help me. In sum, the paper's staff exploited my investigation to intensify its standard reactionary complaints about tenure and allegedly unfit teachers hiding in the school system.

Toward the middle of December, a school district investigator arrived at my school to interview some of my students—ten or fifteen out of about 170 total—and me. He wanted to interview me in my classroom, at least for the first few hours of the total time, in order to take pictures of the many posters on my walls—posters for peace, workers, women, immigrants, human rights all over the world, the environment, wildlife—posters he later described in his "report" with the repeated expression "anti-American." Most of his five and a half hours of questions and follow-up questions were concerned with my political views and protest actions outside the classroom. Before he had finished interviewing me, the principal at my school informed me that "it was in everyone's best interest" that I not teach mass media when school continued after Christmas. From early January to February 21, I taught English classes while the investigator prepared his report supposedly based on the taped interviews of students and me.

The 170-page transcript of the interview bears witness to a teacher and human being infinitely more honest and fair than the investigator's seven-page report portrays. The report accuses me of favoring students who were antiwar and punishing the pro-war ones with low grades and suppression of their dissenting views. In fact, many of the students who did the best in my mass media classes disagreed with the pro-peace perspective I raised and defended in class, a perspective shared by public figures from Noam Chomsky to the Pope. Students' grades were 60 percent participation—meaning the verbalization of something/anything in our discussion of the articles, videos, and other material we used in class. Before our first protest, no student or parent had complained about reading and discussing pro-peace articles in my mass media classes. Even more revealing, according to the investigator himself on tape and now in writing in the transcript in my possession, not one student he interviewed said I was unfair.

In claiming that I provided no "counter-balancing readings or text materials," the investigator ignored materials I presented during the taped de-position. Much of our mass media discussion/activity was based, for example, on Fairness and Accuracy In Reporting's (FAIR's) critiques of TV shows such as *The O'Reilly Factor*. Articles and speeches by Professor Chomsky and others also meticulously presented the perspectives of the *New York Times* and *Wall Street Journal* and other elite opinion makers. The investigator also objected strongly to my use of *Showdown in Seattle,* an unapologetic participant's view of the November 1999 protests against the World Trade Organization. Al-though I told him on tape that I offered extra credit if students wanted to compare the video with corporate media coverage of the same event, he left that fact out of his report to the school board and the public.

Even if half of the investigator's claims of my alleged bias and stifling of pro-war views were indeed true, which they aren't, all any student would have had to do to see dominant views romanticized and valorized would be to step outside my classroom door. There he could easily escape the small world of pro-peace insanity and injustice to reach an Eden of military posters on walls everywhere, Junior ROTC courses and drills, and the ubiquitous military recruiters on campus. The pro-corporate view is not hard to find either—just check out the cafeteria serving Taco Bell and Subway, the Pepsi sun umbrellas on the patio, or the school newspaper, where grades depend on the amount of ad space sold.

In February of 2002, a few days after the investigator's biased, dishonest, misleading report was made public, school superintendent Dan White for-mally reprimanded me, suspended me for three days without pay, and trans-ferred me to adult education full time, away from "impressionable" youth but still influencing "naive" immigrants in Immokalee, according to those people in Naples, including school board member Linda Abbott, who were still trying to get me fired. Not content with local disciplinary measures, the school district forwarded its findings to the state's Professional Practices Services, which will conduct its own investigation and make recommendations that could result in the suspension or revocation of my teaching certificate.

Throughout the months of December, January, and February, and since then as well, I became a professional pariah. Only two or three of my col-leagues would even make eye contact with me, let alone talk to me, and they were my fellow antiwar protesters, who were not under investigation, I suppose, because the district had already made its point. A few teachers did sign a petition circulated by students and presented at a school board meeting before I was suspended. Thankfully, supporters—students, parents, fellow protesters—showed up to speak for me at every school board meeting from the time the investigation started. My teachers' union reps would do nothing more for me than go through the contractual defensive motions; there were no meetings, no rallies, no solidarity. Some union members even objected to the contract's being used to protect me at all.

Recently, in downtown Fort Lauderdale, in front of the federal building, a handful of us held up our coalition banner and two signs that read, "Honk for Peace." The response was inspiring—people flashing the peace sign and thumbs up, and, of course, honking. Some stopped to talk about their doubts that we are doing the right thing by allowing the government, with unquestioned authority, to decide that we will be at perpetual war, killing many people, the majority of whom are poor people of color, women, and kids, for oil and for power, some said. Meanwhile, the poor here at home continue to suffer. Others told us that the politicians can't be trusted, and neither can the corporate media.

This comes as no surprise to those of us out on those corners. We believe there is hope for a better world, but that it begins with all of us as individuals and in concert with as many of us as can be assembled to raise our voices, to keep asking why all human beings cannot live as one and respect the planet and all life in the process. We'll continue to do the same on that corner and on the busy one in Naples where we've stood once a month since December, and where the attacks against me personally all started. War is not the answer. All violence is immoral, whatever its form: poverty, hunger, pollution, rape, prejudice, animal cruelty, unnecessary deaths that could have been prevented with expensive drugs. That message is something all teachers must teach and that all human beings must live.

Ian Harvey can be contacted at mmediamaniac@yahoo.com *or at (239) 353-8929.*

9

Notes from the Trenches

GALEN LEONHARDY

LIVING IN POVERTY WASN'T THE WORST PART FOR GALEN LEONHARDY. Neither was driving miles across the frozen Washington and Idaho countryside on slick tires to take a job as a teacher in an alternative school. But leaving behind his wife and two daughters was hard, even as his family understood that jobs were difficult to come by and that only Leonhardy's passion for transforming the troubled lives of students would keep him company on the long nights between visits. His remarkable journey unfolds through the pages of his journal as we sit in on lessons that empower students, many of whom are running out of options. Leonhardy's insistence on using deliberative, democratic processes as he guides students toward a sense of their own ability and worth meets active and passive resistance from business-as-usual educators and bureaucrats, but his unwavering commitment is a sweet reminder of the power of education and the beauty of a teacher who cares.

August 4, 2000

Today, I left Spokane—my place—my wife, Renee, and my two daughters, Sarah and Hallie, and drove to Kozol Creek, Idaho, where I am setting up classes for the humanities program at a new alternative school. Not being with Renee and the kids is a sacrifice, but it's one I am willing to make. On the one hand, I have the chance to support Renee and the kids financially. We have been poor for many years. On the other hand, I have the chance to construct a process of education that will move students and families who would otherwise be excluded toward inclusion and agency. It is an act of love.

I noticed a sign on the way into town this morning. Painted on an old mill saw that must be at least eight feet in diameter is a woodland scene: green mountains, brown deer, colorful birds, and a couple of pine trees in the foreground. The words on the sign read, "Welcome to Kozol Creek: A Progressive Timber Community." It dawned on me as I drove past the old mill saw that I would likely experience that definition of progressive after I moved into my apartment and started teaching.

August 14, 2000

The temporary space for the faculty and staff of the alternative school is actually a walkway above the main floor of the building. Cheap particleboard tables used as desks are lined up from one end of the walkway to the other end. Visitors come up the stairs, greet me, and then take a left, more often than not walking to the far end where our program manager, Anne Berlin, sits.

Anne currently refuses to allow me to construct my own library of used books for the learner-centered process I proposed during my formal interview. It has been a losing battle. Last month, despite my objections, I was required to order two sets of textbooks with which Anne was familiar. The first set is a series of skill-and-drill workbooks that focus on vocabulary, grammar, and punctuation. Those texts are all based on multiple-choice testing and do not provide opportunities for the students to transfer what they are learning to actual writing. The second set is the kind of texts found in many traditional classrooms. Even though I have not yet read them, I have been asked to put together entire course plans based on the texts. Anne continues to reassure me that I will be allowed to work with the students in the way I had negotiated during my interview, while still telling me that she wants the students to use the skill-and-drill books.

My attempt at a low-key argument has had little influence. This afternoon, I attempted to discuss the textbook issue with Anne from a more academic position, noting that even John Dewey was opposed to an educational diet based solely on "predigested materials" (Ratner, 670). Anne remained passive and did not smile. "The material the students deserve," I pushed on, "needs to be connected to their daily experiences as well as their academic needs, and the problem with the textbooks you are asking me to use is that they are not only distanced from the students' local knowledge but in some cases they are also distanced from actual writing."

Again, Anne's face remained emotionless. She simply stared at me, nodding her head on occasion. I pointed out that Aronowitz and Giroux, for example, argue in *Education Still Under Siege* (1993) that teachers need to gain control over their work conditions, which means, at least in part, that teachers need to move away from such things as nationalized testing and standardized curricula while moving toward teaching practices that are contextually relevant, practices supportive of inclusive opportunities for local knowledge while providing students with the kinds of cultural knowledge that will allow them to gain access to processes of power from which they are excluded (11). "And besides," I continued, "my experiences with resistant students have shown me that approaches outside of the context of their lives simply don't seem to work as well or as rapidly as an individualized process that extends learning by connecting it to their English or history or social studies or whatever the student desires to learn." I ended by noting that Jerome Bruner (1966) recognized that it is impossible for any single curriculum to satisfy the educational needs of any group of children and that an effective curriculum had to provide individualized opportunities (71).

Anne refused to enter into the discussion. After a long silence, she said, "Well, you just finish making these courses, and then we can see if what you want to do will work." Why is my course content being controlled by an administrator? How come well-supported reasoning based on more than one hundred years of educational research has no rhetorical worth in this context? Why did they hire me if they knew that what I wanted to do was not what they wanted to do?

August 24, 2000

With the exception of having a location for the school, Anne and Dr. Fairbanks, the superintendent, had all the pieces together by the time we started this process. The basic foundation for the program included a person who would help the students find employment, three counselors, two teachers, an Americorps volunteer, and an office manager.

On the fifteenth, Anne called the faculty and staff together and took us to visit three possible locations for the alternative school. One turned out to be perfect. It was a research facility surrounded by old-growth cedar and white pine that was located fifteen miles from town. There was the main office, a turn-of-the-century building where Mike, the caretaker of the facility, worked. There were also three log cabins, ranging in size from three to six bedrooms, and there was a fairly large, newly remodeled facility used as a Forest Service classroom for up to thirty people. In addition to the main classroom, the building had four rooms upstairs and a huge kitchen facility with separate dining and cooking areas.

It was a magical place, located less than a mile from a small wilderness area. There were many wonderful opportunities for learning. It was far from town, far from the logging mills, and far enough away that most students would not be able to leave school. It would be a place where students could begin to learn about the ecology of the area. In my mind, it was a place for new beginnings, a place of life and growth.

Serendipity worked in my favor, and after the intense planning period, it was a relief to actually get started down the road to the research facility. Judith's van, loaded with computers and office supplies, led the way on the first trip. She is short, stout, and balding. At sixty-three, she has become an icon of virtue for many in the community. She was also the person selected to teach the math and science classes.

I followed behind her white van in my gray 1981 Datsun diesel, which was filled with my personal library, a substitute for the library I had wanted to construct but could not because Anne forced me to use what limited funds we had on a series of skill and drill workbooks. In addition to becoming an icon of virtue, Judith had also become a cautious driver, which was fine with me because her caution provided opportunities to look around. We drove past the common high school and down a two-lane highway for four or five miles until we passed a sign with "The Hornets' Nest" painted in bright green letters. We turned left and continued down another paved road, passing the Hornets' Nest and then crossing a bridge that spanned a medium-sized river. The road turned to gravel on the other side of the bridge. Dust started coming up through the holes in the floorboard of my truck. I covered the largest hole under the clutch pedal with a pink towel.

As the road wound around, I glanced at the glacier-carved mountains that edged the drainage basin. Then I saw it. Flying low and following the contours at the edge of the valley was a golden eagle, hunting. I grew up going to a Nez Perce sweathouse with my dad. We learned many wonderful things from Nez Perce people, including a little bit of their language. For many Nez Perce, the eagle is an extremely important symbol. Had Judith looked back, she would have seen me swerving all over the road, eventually slowing down to a crawl. Rolling down the window, I watched the eagle as it moved along. From wing tip to wing tip, it was the size of a human. I felt a sense of awe in its presence, but Judith's white van was becoming too distant. I had to continue.

Before long, I caught up to the van. Just as we cleared the top of a rise, however, I saw a second eagle—farther away, more distant. I really only had a short time to watch it between flickering trees and the rise and fall of the road.

Later, I realized the second eagle had been directly over the research facility we were heading toward. The desire to simply stop and watch it was hard to resist, but once again, Judith's van was out of sight. One final glance, and then I returned my focus to the task at hand, saying "*Katz'a yow yow, Quin*" (thank you, Creator) as the moment faded.

The process of unloading and moving took the entire day. We had enough basic materials to get started, but orders would be coming in for some time after the start of school. I spent the weekend away from my family, fixing up the room and getting used to the teaching environment. It is a magnificent room with a high-vaulted ceiling and a wealth of windows offering a view of the forest surrounding the school.

The school itself is much like the brown school I had seen behind Nancie Atwell in a picture on a coffee cup. Her text *In the Middle* (1987) had been a major influence for me. I agreed with Atwell's description of the principles that inform teaching and learning, and had applied those principles with success in alternative settings ranging from detention centers to an alternative program for students who had been expelled or suspended for reasons associated with violence. Atwell provides a reasonable starting point for defining profession-alism in the area of English instruction at all levels. Basically, she holds that writers need regular chunks of time to think, write, confer, read, change their minds, and revise, and writers need to self-select topics of interest. Writers can and will learn about discourse conventions and rules associated with gram-mar and mechanics in context, which is where forms have meaning and value. Atwell also helped me to realize that young writers deserve opportunities to share their writing with adults who write, that writers need to read, and fi-nally, that teachers need to take responsibility for becoming both writers and researchers (17–18). Even though this was only my second full-time teaching position, I knew Atwell's work could be applied at the secondary level, and I knew it could be applied in alternative contexts devoted to serving a wide variety of students who, for a wealth of reasons, were resisting traditional processes.

Many of the resistant youth I have worked with and learned from respond well to the processes of negotiated learning and authentic questioning advo-cated by Atwell. As Atwell puts it, "Adolescents question our adult authority because they are trying to figure out adult reality. They want answers" (35). However, my own experiences with poverty as well as with young people living on the street made me realize that in order to provide answers, we must also recognize the political in what we do.

For that, I turned to the work of a wealth of critical theorists. Peter McLaren's *Life in School: An Introduction to Critical Pedagogy in the Foundations of Education* (1989) was an early source of inspiration. McLaren describes teaching as "a process of inquiry, of critique; it should also be a process of constructing, of building a social imagination that works with a language of hope" (189). By accessing the political, I had discovered that disruptive students could gain opportunities to channel often highly resistant, disruptive, and even self-destructive behaviors toward humanizing activities, toward acts that would not contribute to their own domination.

No tables had been ordered for the classrooms, and we would have been sitting on the floor except Mike Bruzina let us use the narrow desks and padded chairs used for Forest Service meetings. The desks worked well for constructing group tables because they were four feet long, which was a perfect size for two people. In addition, I placed two small tables in the back of the room. In an act of symbolic resistance, I put all of Anne's skill-and-drill textbooks on shelves in the closet at the back of the room and shut the doors. In all, there were enough seats for twenty students, which would be plenty. It was a bright, well-organized room. On Saturday night, I lit sweet grass and *patosway* (a kind of fur), cleansing the room. I also sang four Nez Perce songs that night. I was ready.

August 27, 2000

With so much to do, laundry had been left unfinished back at the apartment. I managed to get back there by noon. The one-bedroom apartment has no covers for any of the lights or windows. It is hollow and lonely. The only real warmth comes from the dishes and coffee cups in the drying rack. My wife, Renee, helped me pick out a couple of cups, a small pot for cooking noodles, and a futon to throw on the floor in the bedroom. Having lived in poverty for many years, we barely had enough money to get the futon, but Renee objected to the idea of my sleeping on the floor every night.

August 30, 2000

Today was the first day of school. It was a hot summer day. Judith and I agreed to start the year off with a lesson she called "Bears in the Woods," which allowed the students to learn about the relationship between resources and population. It was a good lesson in that it included a lot of time outdoors and provided an opportunity for the students to get to know each other.

August 31, 2000

This was actually the first day that I had students in the humanities room. Once they were seated, I asked them to touch their pinkies to their thumbs. All of them did that. Right away, there were pinky-thumb gang signs being flashed all over the place. After the students calmed down a bit, I told them that by virtue of being able to touch their pinkies to their thumbs, they were human. For a moment, a hush fell across the classroom. Nobody had any idea about what I was trying to accomplish.

"So what?" Kane Nelson blurted out.

"So," I responded, "have you ever been in a classroom where the teacher acknowledged that you were human?" I shifted my gaze around the classroom, moving from student to student. Nobody responded. "Well," I continued, "has any teacher ever started a class by pointing out that you are human?" This time several students said that had never happened. "Humm...what does that say about the school system you have been learning in?" Again, there was a long silence. Gina North spoke first.

"It says that the school and the teachers didn't recognize that we are human."

"Okay," I said, "That makes sense to me. But why would that matter to you or me or anybody else?"

Gina continued, "Well, if they didn't recognize that we are humans, then they were taking it away."

"What were they taking away?" I asked her.

"They were taking away our humanness," she said.

"Why is that?" I queried.

Gina replied, "I don't know...maybe it was never something they thought about?"

The rest of the students remained silent. "In this classroom," I said, "the first thing and the last thing we start with is the idea that we all humans. You are human. I am human. We are all human. So we can all learn. You can teach me, and I can teach you. We can all make mistakes. We can all grow. We can reason. We can think about where we live. And because we are all human, we can change. In fact, I think we can change the world if we work together."

Together, we read and briefly discussed the first chapter from *Angela's Ashes*, a book about a child who was raised in Ireland and who later immigrated to the U.S. After that, they received their first writing assignment, which I told them would count as a journal entry. After the short writing assignment, I told them that the only required assignment would be a daily journal entry. In order to get credit for any class that I taught, every day each student had to write at least a one-page entry that would remain private.

For this first writing assignment, which would count as their first journal entry, I asked the students to tell me something important about themselves, something that would help me to know what they thought was important. Immediately, students began writing. After the initial sounds of backpacks thumping on desks, zippers, and three-ring binders being opened, the only audible sound was the ruffling of paper. In the middle of that very active silence, Lucy Leuchtenburg cleared her throat and raised her hand.

"May I help you?" I asked.

"Yeah," Lucy responded in a loud, croaking voice, "do you want to hear about the time I lost my fucking virginity?"

The class erupted. Some laughed. Others yelled encouragement. A few students pounded on their desks. I smiled and felt a flush of embarrassment cross my cheeks. Once the uproar quieted, I cleared my throat and said, "Well, to be perfectly honest, I think that would be a bit personal for this assignment. But the question is, why would you want to write about that?" Like everybody else, Lucy remained silent, so I continued, saying, "Until you know why you would want to write about something like that to somebody who is at this point little more than a stranger, I would be inclined to say that it is a bit personal."

The rest of the day was spent handing out the texts Anne is requiring me to use. However, in addition to checking out books, I made it a point to find out what each student wanted to do, which was a direct and overt departure from Anne's curriculum. I have made the choice to work against habit and myth.

Many of the students did not know what they wanted to do. More than half, however, already had contemplated possible areas of study and even possible projects. Perhaps the most aggressive plan came from Gina North, who told me that she wanted to graduate by Christmas so she could enroll in a college and get a degree that would allow her to support herself and her son without having to rely on money from the welfare system. In order to accomplish that goal, Gina would have to finish six classes in addition to enrolling in college and applying for financial aid. I said that I would be willing to help her achieve that goal if she was willing to help construct her own education. She understood that the promise of collaboration was not necessarily a promise to finish early.

October 12, 2000

Each month, we are supposed to have a steering committee meeting. This one produced some surprising news. It seems Dr. Fairbanks, the superintendent, wants to move the school to the Panhandle Mill. What kind of place is this Panhandle Mill and why wasn't I introduced to this idea prior to the monthly meeting? More important, why weren't the students introduced to the place? That is, Dr. Fairbanks is planning on moving the school in the near future to a new location, and as far as I can tell, nobody else has been a part of the decision-making process.

October 15, 2000

Today, the teachers, faculty, and staff went to visit our new "home." The Panhandle Mill is an old warehouse and loading dock for grain and animals. Cows, horses, wheat, and by all indications a fair amount of mice and rats were stored at the mill and then loaded onto trains for delivery to Spokane and other cities. In addition to rodent droppings, there are large holes in the walls and many nails needing to be pounded back into the boards from which they sprang. The outside is covered with a faded red. I started calling it "the barn." Democracy is not so much about voting as it is about problem-solving processes mediated through dialogue and other active forms of collaboration. I will push for democracy.

October 16, 2000

After school, Anne called a meeting. At one point, she asked me what I thought about the new location and the idea of moving. I noted that the process needed to include both students and parents because they were being excluded. "The process is not democratic." I continued, "It is authoritarian." I then pointed out that the Research Institute had been an extremely beneficial place for students. After noting through clenched teeth that she would find out if we had any options, Anne abruptly pushed herself away from the table and stomped out of the room, leaving the rest of us staring at each other in surprise. Though Anne was not happy when I brought up the ideas of dialogue and democracy, she did come around to the idea of representation.

October 18, 2000

Three weeks ago, I started preparing the teachers and staff for my showing of *Schindler's List*. Extreme racism plagues our daily interactions, especially among the male students. From that perspective, it has taken me nearly two months to get this group of students to the point where I felt comfortable watching the movie with them.

Loren Watkins told me before class started that she had a friend who just died. Somehow the death is related to heroin use. Loren is in a constant state of panic—wide eyes, fidgety movements, quickly agitated. She is difficult to reach, almost impossible to connect with in a way that would sustain academic interactions. Anne, Bertha (the intern and primary counselor), and Judith have all mentioned and spent a good deal of time talking about the idea that Loren is "sexually active." I am not sure why their focus is on that issue. I am more worried about the fact that Loren is a traumatized child.

What is my role as a teacher in relation to Loren's experiences? Certainly, it is a process of negotiation and dialogue. Still, I am not sure what to do. Too often, discussions among the adults here are voyeuristic, focusing on the sexual relations kids have. *Schindler's List* has much to say to viewers about the need to question the processes that support oppression. To do so, we must recognize that the children and families we serve often experience combat zone realities. Obviously, deconstructing such realities requires more than gossiping about sexual interactions. Real alternatives require moving students, parents, faculty, staff, and communities toward democracy and dialogue while supporting local knowledge and working against delusional reasoning.

October 20, 2000

One of our students, Donna, just finished a whole semester's worth of English. Her family does not have a phone, so I ended my day by going downtown to the bar where Donna's mom, Bernadette, works. Bernadette, who could just as easily be working in the woods with a saw as tending bar, laughed and bought me a beer. Her connection to the place goes back six generations. Mary Ann and Donna, her two daughters, make the seventh generation to grow up in the Kozol Creek area. We talked for nearly an hour.

It's a dark bar—colored lights, blues and reds, some green. There was the sound of pool balls and people talking. I sat on a stool, "bellied up" to the bar, as Bernadette described it. The conversation was completely focused on what her kids were doing and how they were affected by the school and its current location. Shortly before I left, Bernadette told me I was the only teacher who did not intimidate her. Thank goodness. That was at about 9:50 P.M., and I was thinking about getting back to my little white futon. It felt empowering to know that Bernadette agreed with me about "the barn." Eventually, there was a handshake and a walk to the solid wooden door. Then there was night air, the sound of my truck, the door to the apartment, the futon, and the sounds of logging trucks and chains.

October 23, 2000

I met with Lori Smith's mom, Jan, after school. Their house is located between the school and the highway. They live next to the Hornets' Nest, the backwoods bar and greasy spoon that first caught my attention the day I saw the eagle. Lori's mom met me at the door to their trailer. We shook hands as I introduced myself and explained why I was knocking on her trailer door, saying that Lori had been absent for the seventh time in less than three weeks. Most of the absences were because Lori had physical therapy. They just hadn't called.

Before she left this afternoon, Anne had told me Lori's absences were because of drug use. It seemed reasonable to find out what was going on. There is another issue with gossip or speculation that this incident points to.

Lori's mom called for Lori. I spoke with Lori for a few minutes at the door, thinking I would end the conversation with a question about her homework. Lori paused, then admitted she had not been keeping up the "Green Sheets," one of several monitoring forms. "Well, Lori, if you let me in, I can show you how to deal with those things."

Lori studies in her "study room." One of the walls in the room has graffiti on it. There are several that say Kozol Creek Crips. There is also a desk and a chair. Beyond that, the room, like the rest of the trailer, is piled with fallen stacks of papers and magazines and blankets and shoes. Lori sat in the chair and I knelt beside her, which is exactly what I do when the students are sitting at their tables in the humanities room. Lori had all her work out and ready to go. I made sure she had enough hours to get by for full-time attendance, and then we started into history.

Lori told me she did not know anything about history. So I asked her about the Hornets' Nest. Lori knew much about the bar. I have heard from my next-door neighbor that youth can get into the bar and buy beer. Lori would not admit that, saying only that she spent time at the bar eating food and talking to people. It was fairly easy to convince her that a history unit could be constructed that would allow her to write about the history of the bar. That appealed to Lori because she spent so much time there.

Lori and her mom wanted to know why a history of the Hornets' Nest would be important. They smiled and actually got excited when I pointed out that they had both been studying the bar for seven years and that their knowledge of the bar was a legitimate historical study. I ended there, pointing out that as an academic, I was far more interested in Lori and Jan's knowledge of the area than I was about Christopher Columbus or the founding fathers. The local knowledge about a bar in the middle of the woods seemed more relevant to me, especially since a mother and daughter had been collaboratively studying the bar for the last seven years.

I spent a good deal of time moving Lori and her mom toward understanding that the way history was traditionally taught subjugated local knowledge. Lori noted that her mom did not like the Hornets' Nest. Though I had a reasonable guess as to the reason, I asked Lori why. She frowned, saying the bar was a "drug place." Lori said she did not like that influence either. "So take a stand," I encouraged her. "If you don't think it is right for the people at the bar to sell drugs, say that in your research paper."

In addition, I asked Jan if she knew the steering committee was planning to move the school. Her comment was that she thought the Panhandle Mill had been condemned. As I left the trailer, Jan shook my hand, saying, "Thanks for stopping." I was grateful for her being receptive to this sort of contact between a teacher and her family.

October 26, 2000

Today, the students had a class meeting. I don't usually get to hear much of what they say. The meetings are for them. But most of the time, students tell me about the issues they address. This time, Lucy told me they talked about a wide range of issues, including drug use at school. They also talked about classroom behavior, respect, sexual intercourse, stealing (especially cigarettes), and a variety of issues.

It is important to help students understand the connection between their actions and theory. As I do with most students, Lucy and I extended the conversation. In this case, we talked about the need for communication and community building in relation to her being the steering committee representative for students. Her approach has been to engage the school community with dialogue—and the community is responding with dialogue. In that process, there is a significant step for youth who have been subjected to such a focused experience within the predatory culture that surrounds them. Like Lucy, I am satisfied that the students are using dialogue. They are communicating.

During the showing of *Schindler's List*, I spoke about how Schindler only had language to use in his resistance. In the face of all the violence, Schindler had nothing but his voice. When the students at the alternative school gather to engage in dialogue, for example, I know something powerful is happening. Radical democracy takes time. We can't get it in a hurry. Dialogue offers alternatives to the combat zone reality these youth face on a daily basis. Democracy, compassion, and collaboration require dialogue. But I would be foolish to think these youth will suddenly and miraculously change overnight. It took years of social processes to construct the youth in these combat zones. It will likely take years not just to help the youth in this school learn that they can work on the world but also to change the social reality that surrounds us. We have to be savvy about this. If we are going to act with love, we must also act with reason. We need to recognize that the webs of interaction that surround us will not change soon and that the construction of alternatives requires steady resistance.

We also need to know what students experience. Of the thirty students, several have family members who have been murdered. Some have been shot at. Nearly all of the female students have experienced attempted rapes or have been raped. One was left for dead in a ditch. Another was raped by her stepfather. Drug use is also common. According to one Department of Social and Health Services (DSHS) caseworker I know, the increase in drug manufacturing that followed a radical decrease in the availability of welfare funding made meth one of the area's leading exports. If students are getting raped at home, they need to be able to talk about it. If they have to fight their parents, they need to be able to talk about it. If they are dealing with drugs, they need to be able to talk about it. And it is our responsibility to support and protect that process.

That is why it is powerful that the students are discussing issues like drug use on campus or sexual intercourse or whatever they want to discuss. They are reasoning with honesty. They are talking about things that limit them. They are talking as a collective striving for collective action. They are taking some control of and for their own educational processes with reasoned and relevant dialogue, something that has been missing from their educational and social realities.

November 1, 2000

Today we had a steering committee meeting. Gina North represented the students in Lucy's place. Gina picked two student issues and presented them well. Her argument was that 90 percent of the students did not want to move from the research station and that the students wanted on-site daycare.

Dr. Fairbanks told the committee the daycare could not become a reality because it was a local business area, so the school would be competing against business owners. I thought about how I was going to have to find a lawyer to check that idea out. He never says how he knows these things. Gina noted there were only eight mothers at the school and that most of them could not afford daycare anyway. I then brought up the idea that calling it a daycare might be a misnomer. What we were constructing could be better described as collaborative child-raising because the students planned to take turns raising the children. Moreover, we were not competing with local daycare providers because we were neither charging for the service nor actively seeking to attract parents whose children were not part of the program. Anne noted that we might want to have a local daycare provider come in and teach the students about running an effective daycare. Dr. Fairbanks shut down the dialogue, saying simply, "There will be no daycare at this point."

The discussion then focused on the prospect of moving the school. Dr. Fairbanks presented his reasons for the move. I kept thinking that the process was not collaborative. Gina waited and then politely restated that 90 percent of the students did not want to move. Without so much as a glance at her, Dr. Fairbanks started talking about the process of moving to the barn. Another committee member, Stan Lowman, filled up any empty space that would have allowed Gina to respond. And the conversation would have ended there if I had kept silent. "I think what I heard Gina say was that 90 percent of the students do not want to make the move." That stopped the conversation. I have heard the condition called a pregnant silence, and that is exactly what it was.

Dr. Fairbanks focused his gaze on Gina and spoke to her about the difficulty of not moving, citing high transportation costs, slow Internet connections, insufficient heating systems, and inadequate space.

Of course, his reasons are *his* reasons. There has been nothing collaborative about this process. Additionally, none of those reasons is sufficient to support moving without collaborative interactions. Everything is working fine, and it would cost more to rebuild the barn than it would to stay at the research station, even if we all do as Dr. Fairbanks is requesting and spend our Christmas vacation getting the barn fixed up.

Again, in his interaction with Gina, he left no room for discussion. Rather than mentoring, he was playing to win against a sixteen-year-old. Unfortunately, Gina had to leave soon after that. After she left, I spoke about how important it was that the students were participating as stakeholders and how important it was for us to acknowledge their participation. The idea I presented to the committee members was that if we were going to support and include students, we needed to treat them as humans capable of understanding and disagreeing and collaboratively constructing the school with us. Stan said, "Well, maybe we could take them down to the mill to see the place."

I need to make a mountain out of that molehill. Success comes in small doses in the movement toward radical democracy. Stan made a major concession by mediating a position about the relationship between teachers and students. Without that compromise, we would have been doing little more than continuing the oppression these youth, and their parents in many cases, have endured for years. I want more than that, but for now much has been accomplished. And interestingly enough, part of the reason Stan decided to support the students was connected to Gina's well-articulated and well-thought-out position. She held her own in a context with which she has little experience.

It is night and I am alone again in this one-room flat. I found out that Susan Hawkins' current boyfriend also rented this same apartment. She is fifteen. He is twenty-one and also the father of Brenda Cox's three-year-old son (Brenda attends classes on Fridays, as does Susan, who is often driven to school by her boyfriend). He has three other children as well. It is a strange connection. He now lives about two blocks from here.

As for me, I am currently looking for another place to live, because the baseboard heat will be too expensive for me to use. Goodness, after fourteen years of college, I can't make a loan payment, and I will most likely not be able to turn on the heat in the apartment. I mention that because tonight, for the first time, I turned on the heat. I had been blowing steam with every breath from the time I got home until I took my "seminightly" walk. I turned on the heat before I left, and now that I am home, it is starting to get warm.

November 5, 2000 (Sunday)

I worked with Saundra Jennings, an independent study student. Last Friday, I read to her from the first few pages of *Discipline and Punish* by Foucault. I decided to do that because Saundra "wasn't being challenged." After reading until *she* had had enough of Foucault's challenging ideas, I summarized the discussion on how power is maintained. Together, Saundra and I synthesized Foucault's patterns of power maintenance in the prison complex to power maintenance in schools and classrooms.

It has taken a lot of work to move the students toward recognizing the reality of economic oppression. Both Anne and Judith keep telling them that education will make it so they will not be poor. And Anne keeps pushing the nationalism. But the students are starting to ask questions. Many are reading the articles I hand them when we talk about the complex ideas related to social justice.

November 6, 2000

Gina North is reading Paulo Freire's *Pedagogy of the Oppressed*. She finished Machiavelli's *The Prince* and Kozol's *Amazing Grace*. I keep reminding myself that she started the year asking me if she could pursue a course of study that would allow her to graduate at the end of the year, mentioning family hardship and the need to support her son on her own as reasons for wanting to make the attempt. The collaboration was not so complex then as it is now. What started with Gina spread to others. There are students doing all sorts of things now, especially since they have witnessed a comrade's success and have engaged in dialogue with that person.

November 8, 2000

Today, we had to give the Idaho Aptitude Test—more stuff working against the possibility of democracy in our classrooms. If only this test could show that students here are capable of discussing Foucault or Paulo Freire. If only the test could show what the students know about the Hornets' Nest and how that connects to research and history.

I did what I always do with these tests. I introduced the test and then discussed the reasons I cannot support this sort of testing process. It is a form of resistance that allows me to explore alternative forms of assessment with students while moving them toward the recognition that assessment and instruction should inform and influence one another, that assessment should be collaboratively constructed and contextually relevant.

The resistance, however, is not so extreme that someone could remove me from my teaching assignment. Today, there was a nice discussion prior to the test in which several students talked about the negative experiences they had with other standardized tests. After that, I moved the class into the testing process. After all of the stressful interactions with Anne, I did not feel safe going over specific questions, taking on the test as a class. When we model resistance, we should show the students savvy rather than self-limiting forms of resistance.

Both Don Liner and Kyle Ramage drew Christmas trees by coloring in the dots. It was resistance. However, as I noted, their actions did not indicate they had learned how to take these kinds of tests. Their resistance, which was a fairly safe form of resistance in this case, would be self-limiting in situations where this testing process was used to establish hierarchies and provide access to economic security.

To make matters worse, however, Don would finish a section and then start walking around the class and out the door. Reminding him about his commitments and expectations had no effect. So I asked for Anne to work with him. Anne provided no support. She simply talked to him once and then ignored what he was doing after that. My choices, then, were to chase after him while he literally ran around the building or to give the test. I have told Anne several times that the students need clear expectations.

Eventually, I went over to the math and science area to see if Judith was ready for a break. When I went over to see her, little, white-haired, Irish woman from Boston that she is, I found her actively coaching the students through the test and supporting a collaborative process of answering standardized questions. I told her later that she was my inspiration. She beamed. The students, by the way, were having a blast.

I also told Judith I was too afraid for my job to have gone as far with my resistance. Anne had specifically told me to give the test as it was written. Then Trudy (the office manager) came into my room and silently watched me as I was discussing the reasons many scholars in assessment do not support standardized tests. I felt a bit self-conscious. Oh, and then Ruby Kerford, the JOBS coordinator, entered the room and loudly engaged Donna Sagal, attempting to make her take another test for the online classes. The interruption was one thing. Moving a student away from one worthless test for another was a source of consternation.

These kinds of interruptions have become common practice for both Ruby and Anne. I decided to continue the test while Ruby argued with the student. It was nearly unreal. In fact, I would have considered it silliness except every time I pointed out something about a question or helped a student learn test-taking skills, Ruby would physically and visibly cringe. I had to guess what her body signs indicated. In the end, I was just not feeling safe enough to turn the test into a collective activity.

Seeing that Judith was doing what I wanted to do, however, helped me feel more secure about making a shift in that direction. After break, I returned to the room and engaged the test *with* the students. The process became collaborative and formative. Don Liner and Kyle Ramage continued to maintain disruptive resistance, coloring in their tests randomly and laughing. Moving close to their table, I quieted them, and while the other students were working, I asked

Don to explain why he was refusing to take part in the sort of resistance that would at least let the class engage as a community of learners in a collaborative process. Don growled that my ideas were fucked, that school was stupid, and that he was tired of all the shit he had to put with. Then he asked me why I thought learning was so important.

I explained that the information passed on in schools was important because it allowed him access to information that made economic stability and inclusion more likely. If any of them resisted in ways that supported their own illiteracy, especially extreme forms such as not reading, they would be resisting in a way that would support their own oppression.

Smiling at Don, I continued, noting that if he continued to resist by not reading or by refusing to engage schoolwork, he would stand the chance of moving himself to the point that he would not even know he was getting stomped on by social forces. I went on to say that I did not want that to happen because I recognized his humanness. As a human, I could not contribute to his oppression willingly. "So," I continued, "what we are trying to do with this test is make the best of the situation."

The first snow fell today. We had more than two inches by the time I left from Spokane where I went to vote. Renee called her dad and asked if he would help us buy new tires for the truck. "The Beast," as I call my 1981 Datsun Diesel King Cab, is almost twenty years old. The tires are nearly bald, a deadly way to travel down the back roads of northern Idaho. This morning, while returning from the two-hour trip back to Spokane, I almost didn't make it. Between Spokane and Kozol Creek, there is a snow belt stretching from Riverside to Newport, Washington. There was more than an inch of snow on the road. With no weight in the back and no studs, I was all over the road.

Part of the problem is that the alignment is shot. That will be yet another expense we can't afford. As I was spinning across the highway into oncoming traffic, I remember thinking and laughing to myself because I realized in the middle of a spin that what I suffered from was blinding poverty in a blinding snowstorm. The big trucks managed to miss me, and I stayed on the side of the road until my heart stopped pounding. I did not tell Renee about that incident.

The kids at the school know I do not have much money. I am honest with them when they ask why I wait for them before I get leftovers from school lunch and breakfast. I wish more of them recognized their own poverty as well.

I told Linda Black her photography assignment was to make images of poverty. Linda did not know what "poverty" meant. I told her poverty could mean many things, but that what I was thinking about was economic hardship. Linda then told me the assignment was "stupid" because there wasn't any poverty to photograph around Kozol Creek. I pointed out that she and her mom were living in Kozol Creek's only subsidized housing unit, that the poverty she could not find was right at her doorstep. Linda repeated that the assignment was stupid, but she was not able to elaborate beyond that when I asked to explain what she meant. Still, she kept the camera with her and asked several other students what they thought poverty was and how she could photograph it.

She is not the only student to become outraged at that particular assignment. Many of the youth share a denial of the poverty that exists around them. Their own poverty is seldom recognized. Seldom is their suffering acknowledged. I work not only to affirm the reality of their poverty but also to move them toward agency.

The Election Day conversation started when several students, including Linda, noted that they did not think they could have any influence on the world. I responded by talking about the movie *Schindler's List*. That turned the tide. I then brought up the idea that even if several students did not think they could work on the world as individuals, the community as a whole could do what individuals could not do. That is, the students began to see that they have become a community and that they are already involved in social action.

All in all, things are going fairly well. Most of the youth are focused on individual projects, and most seem to be finding success. They have become a community that uses dialogue rather than violence. They talk about important issues, relevant to their daily lives, and the collective process they have learned to use often results in individual or small-group activism that will become a powerful force in the larger community. Still, as the evening comes to an end, I can't help but think about Renee and the kids. Though I am trying to make the world a better place for our children, I can't help but miss my family.

It is a dark moon on a snowy night.

Works Cited

Aronowitz, Stanley and Henry A. Giroux. 1993. *Education Still Under Siege.* London: Bergin and Garvey.

Atwell, Nancie. 1987. *In the Middle: Writing, Reading, and Learning with Adolescents.* Portsmouth, NH: Boynton/Cook.

Bruner, Jerome S. 1966. *Toward a Theory of Instruction.* London: Belknap/Harvard.

Freire, Paulo. 1997. *Pedagogy of the Oppressed.* New York: Continuum Publishing.

Foucault, Michel. 1977. *Discipline and Punish: The Birth of the Prison.* Trans. Alan Sheridan. New York: Vintage Books.

Kozol, Jonathan. 1995. *Amazing Grace*. New York: HarperCollins.

Machiavelli, Niccolo. 1981. *The Prince*. Trans. George Bull. London: Penguin Books.

McCourt, Frank. 1996. *Angela's Ashes*. New York: Scribner.

McLaren, Peter. 1989. *Life in Schools: An Introduction to Critical Pedagogy in the Foundations of Education*. New York and London: Longman.

Ratner, Joseph. 1939. *Intelligence in the Modern World: John Dewey's Philosophy*. New York: Random House.

In addition to teaching in Idaho, Galen Leonhardy worked as a substitute teacher at several detention centers and volunteered at Crosswalk, a shelter for street youth in Spokane, Washington. He now teaches at Black Hawk College in Moline, IL.

10

Words Can Never Hurt Me

CISSY LACKS

WHEN DR. CISSY LACKS JOINED THE FACULTY OF BERKELEY HIGH SCHOOL IN 1992, in one of three high schools in the Ferguson-Florissant School District in St. Louis, she brought with her a long and distinguished record of professional achievement and recognition for herself and her students. During her more than twenty years in this district, her students had won national awards for excellence in scholastic journalism and creative writing. The Dow-Jones Newspaper Fund named her as one of the top fifteen newspaper advisers in the country. Despite her credentials and accomplishments, and the universal acclaim accorded her by students, Lacks was fired in March of 1995 for allowing her students to write drama exercises that included dialogue natural to the characters they created. She sued the school district on counts relating to the First Amendment and race discrimination. Her case became one of the most disturbing in the annals of school law.

---

*N*a... Na... NaNa... Na. *Sticks and stones can break my bones but words will never hurt me.* I heard that childhood chant shouted across the schoolyard almost every day of my grade school life. It was a first and early defense against a verbal attack.

But as almost everyone knows, even children who yell the response, it is just not true. Words are mighty. What hardly anyone ever says, because no catchy chant could express it, is that as powerful as words are, the ones censored can cause more harm than those spoken.

As a teacher of English and journalism for twenty-seven years, I knew the childhood proclamation was wrong, appreciated the power of words, and didn't censor student writing for fear of the inevitable damage it caused later.

In all those years, no one particularly cared to know what I was doing, how I felt about teaching or what I thought about words. But in one day, that situation changed dramatically. On that day, and then for days, months, and years afterward, my teaching, as well as my personal life, received more attention than I ever could have imagined.

I was Person of the Week for ABC News, the cover for *Teacher Magazine*, a show topic for *Dateline NBC* and recipient of the prestigious PEN First Amendment Award.

I could have been participating in a most honored and affirming retirement—except I was not retired; I was fired. Fired for listening to my students. And perhaps as important, fired for listening to my students because they were one race and I was another.

In a confrontation over words, I was the collateral damage. What happened to me is a teacher's nightmare, but the real victims were then and continue to be students in classrooms across the United States and, yes, even around the world.

I almost didn't check my answering machine the night it all started. It was 10 P.M. when I got home from dinner and the movies, late for a teacher who had to be up at 6 A.M. and in her classroom ready to go by 7:10. I pushed the play button more out of habit than curiosity.

> Hello, Cissy. This is Mr. Mitchell, and the time now is 7:53. I would like to talk with you regarding the tape that was done about two or three weeks ago involving your class, and I have viewed it. I intended to talk with you earlier with regard to who has the tape. It's pretty shocking and I would like for you to meet me at the administration building tomorrow morning at 8:30. There is no need for you to report to the school, I have them covered. You need to report to the administration building at 8:30 A.M. Thank you.

I thought about the message on my machine. *The tape was pretty shocking.* I didn't know what he was talking about, even after I thought about it and thought about it, all night, almost every minute of all night.

It turned out the tape was one my students had worked on three months before, a tape of drama exercises they had written as the culmination of a drama unit. The drama exercises were first, sometimes awkward, attempts by students who took themselves and the assignment seriously. And yes, they did use street language, and sometimes lots of it, in the dialogue they created for their characters.

At that 8:30 A.M. meeting, I was suspended—a decision that had been made before I arrived. Two months later, I was fired.

In the twenty-five years that I taught creative writing, twenty of them in this same school district, I had never thought nor been told to censor my students' writing. When students were serious about communicating what they or their characters were thinking, they needed to choose the words without someone else telling them what words to choose. This teaching method—allowing students their voices and then teaching them how to be most effective with their voices—is practiced in classrooms all over the United States.

In my case, no one ever had directed me to teach otherwise. In fact, I had been rewarded and acknowledged as a successful and talented creative writing teacher for using the very same method now cited as the reason I should be fired. My personnel file contained many complimentary letters and awards, and not one single complaint in all the years I had worked in the district.

The issue wasn't really words. The issue really was whether I, or any teacher, should censor students' creative thoughts and expressions and whether I, or any teacher, could be fired without notice because someone took offense at what was produced in a classroom assignment—even though numerous classes over several years had learned to write through this same process and method with great success and without complaint.

It didn't take long to find out that words were only one motive for my firing. That the concerns of the principal were more about race than about words was reflected in a comment he made to one student about the drama exercises:

And when I look at that tape, I see black students acting a fool, OK? And I see white folks videotaping it, OK? Did you think about that . . . ?

My students wrote their scripts after watching a television interview of a Pulitzer Prize–winning playwright giving advice on writing. "Write about things important to you and write from authentic voices you hear in your lives," he said.

I told them: "If you want to see yourself on tape, if you want to see how you project yourself, we can tape these productions. But I want to tell you that I know it takes some guts to look at yourself and critique yourself and the only people who will look at the tape are the students in our two classes."

We had nothing to hide. Many people, including parents and administrators, had sat in on my classes, observing works in progress with my students' knowledge and agreement. Also, I encouraged students to perform work publicly, when they and I thought it was ready. In this instance, the school district made the decision to show my students' work in public. They showed the very tapes that I had promised my students would not be shown outside our two classes. The school administrators did not ask permission of my students, their parents, or me. After the school district confiscated the tapes, the tapes somehow were made available to local TV stations and soon were broadcast on the major networks. In addition to my case being about respect for teachers and for students, it was also about important educational issues such as rights to privacy and safe, time-out places in classrooms. It was about trust between students and teachers.

In a subsequent meeting with the three administrators—the principal of the high school, Vernon Mitchell; assistant superintendent of personnel, John Wright; and an assistant superintendent of curriculum, Barbara Davis—who initiated the termination charges against me, I offered an example to illustrate the power and potential of words for a student's intellectual growth. A student in one of my classes at Berkeley High School walked into my class every day, went to the back of the room, and put his head on a desk. He was disconnected from me, from school, from learning, and probably from himself. But inside him was a poet that even he didn't know about, and when we started writing poetry in class, he couldn't resist joining in. The first two exercises he read aloud fired out like an unaimed shotgun—exploding with street language, gang slang, and anger. Less than three weeks later he wrote a poem that won a district award and had his fellow students and me in tears:

ALONE
I'm all alone in the world today.
No one to laugh with, no one to play.
It's been like that since the age of three.
No one to love, care or hold me.
I guess that's why I'm the way I am.
No one loved me so I don't give a damn.
No one to pick me up when I fall.
No one to measure growth or how tall.
Alone how it hurts inside.
If I were to die, no one would cry.
I never gave a damn about any other.
I love my shoes
More than I love my mother.
You might think I'm the Devil or call me Satan.
I have no love I'm so full of haten.
I guess that's why I have low self esteem.
The only time I show love
Is in my dreams.

—*Reginald McNeary*

Two days later, my attorney told me that these administrators had added a charge of profanity in poetry and had submitted as evidence Reginald's first two poems. They had ignored and discarded Reginald's final poem that had been published and had won awards. These administrators said they didn't remember having seen it. They totally ignored the process of teaching and they totally ignored the results of the process. Why would people entrusted with the responsibility to educate children do such a thing to me or anyone else?

At my hearing before the school board, one of my students testified that profanity was part of her life and the characters she wrote into the scripts came from people in her life. She said that she appreciated the opportunity to write about life as she saw it without being censored. She shared what she learned from completing the exercise, which included her explanation of how important it was for her and her classmates to care about what they were doing and to believe that what they were writing and the skills they were learning had a value in their lives.

When my student was finished, a school board member asked her, "If things could be different for you, would you like them to be? . . . What I was getting at, if you are in a situation where you don't want to be, like you were saying black, African community, that's the way it is, is profanity, where do we begin to change that . . . ?"

My student looked right at this board member and said, "I like the way my life is now," and added a few minutes later, "My mother raised me right. If you don't disrespect me, I won't disrespect you."

My student knew what the school board member had yet to comprehend. People of all ages have different ways of speaking in different circumstances. Teenagers are no different from anyone else. Even more important, realities in people's lives are not the same; yet, some people are neither willing nor capable of understanding or facing the differences. They would rather live with the lie that everything is just fine for everyone. If they admitted otherwise, they might have to deal with the circumstances that weren't so fine.

This creative writing assignment and this teaching method in a high school in St. Louis County, Missouri, received national interest as soon as the controversy hit the wire services. And it didn't receive attention because some student creative writing had street language in the dialogue. Why I became a lightning rod is connected to a complex set of factors involving race, school politics, cultural struggles, teachers' roles, authority concerns, denial mechanisms, power issues, and numerous other influences and stresses in our society. No matter what circumstances were stirring the pot, one premise should have been of utmost importance: Teaching students to understand voice would help them know who they were and that self-knowledge would enable them to find a place for themselves in the world. A classroom of students was learning how to communicate to others and themselves about who they were and what happened in their lives. Because some people might not like hearing what the students had to say, or how they said it, was no reason to stop the conversation. The entire country seemed to recognize the importance of this issue.

At the school board hearing, the Ferguson-Florissant School District submitted Reginald's first two poems and the taped drama exercises to justify my dismissal. They did not submit Reginald's award-winning poem, and they would not recognize my success in the classroom. While some people may have been taken aback by my students' dialogue and Reginald's first poems, many more were amazed by the district's repudiation of its own curriculum directives for teaching writing in the Ferguson-Florissant School District— curriculum directives that I followed.

The district's written instructions to teachers included the following:

Don't tell writers what should be in their writing or, worse, write on their pieces.

Build on what writers know and have done, rather than bemoaning what's not on the page or what's wrong with what is there.

Resist making judgments about the writing.

In questioning students, ask about something you're curious about as an inquisitive human being.

And this astonishment grew even greater when I explained that the official grounds cited for firing me had nothing to do with curriculum or instruction. I was accused of disobeying an appendix to the student discipline code, that appendix being the only place in any school board regulation that mentioned profanity. Some examples of student behavior that would be in violation of this type of regulation are tardiness, unexcused absence, leaving school grounds without permission, littering, profanity, insubordination, inappropriate dress, and lying to school authorities. Punishment for a student who was determined to have violated this appendix might be nothing more than a talking to or, in the most severe instances, a ten-day suspension. Several district teachers and administrators testified that no teacher would expect that an appendix to a student discipline code could be construed in any way as the basis for disciplining a teacher, nor could it be applied to students as they were involved in instructional activities.

Kangaroo court was in session. Many observers likened my six-day hearing to the Scopes "monkey trial."

Even worse than ignoring its own policies was the lie the district used to "prove" that previously I had been warned about the use of profanity.

According to state and federal law, as well as the Ferguson-Florissant teachers' contract, teachers must be given a fair warning if the district believes a teacher is acting in violation of a district policy. Disciplinary action can be taken if the cited behavior continues after this warning. No one had ever warned me to censor my students' language, but so what? The board, the administrators, and the lawyers were all working together. If someone made up something, it was true if the decision makers said it was. It was a game of the emperor's new clothes. One of the lies made up by the principal was, and is still, my worst nightmare of the case. Although I would have the satisfaction of seeing him forced to answer for his lies in federal court, later I learned that he would be allowed to get away with them.

If I could have looked ahead in time to my court case, and then returned to the beginning, when the district was accusing me, I would have known my story was the same as the myriad of stories like mine in schools everywhere. Good teachers trying to work effectively with their students were getting trapped in our country's culture wars. Learning fields had become mined battlefields, but it was going to take my case, and some others, and a handful of catastrophic school violence incidents before most teachers would understand how vulnerable they were, and how ineffective this new censorship dogma would render them. The public's awareness of the culture wars playing out in our public schools was even further behind than the teachers'. At the moment I was attacked by the school district, it was to be expected that my supporters and I did not know what this turmoil was all about. We were sure it wasn't my students' tapes that were the issue but we couldn't have imagined what it really was, either. But we would learn, learn more than anyone would want to know.

I was stunned at the intimidation and bullying perpetrated by these administrators in their meetings with me. After all, I had worked with these people for over twenty years. I chose to have a public hearing, and, when I sued the Ferguson-Florissant School District, a public trial. I believed an open hearing with the opportunity to examine district administrators was the only way these administrators and the school board could be made accountable for their behavior.

The morning I was called in and summarily suspended, one assistant superintendent ending the meeting by saying I should "Go home and do nothing," suggesting in her tone that I wasn't good for anything else. At that meeting, none of the three would tell me what tapes they were talking about, and I didn't know. When I did find out, they refused to let me see my classes' drama tapes upon which they were basing their actions, even though the tapes had been just one of many classroom exercises done three months earlier. These three administrators also tried to intimidate my students. They tape-recorded interviews of some of the students in those classes, refusing to let us attend the interviews, and then submitted, to their attorneys and us, inaccurate summaries to help their case. The three administrators denied that actual tapes existed. When students insisted the conversations were recorded, the district was forced to relinquish the audiotapes in response to my attorney's legal request.

The principal had confiscated the student tapes from my locked class-room closet, but other items were taken as well. One of them was my grade book. And, at a meeting called by these administrators supposedly to listen to my explanation of the situation, the assistant superintendent of personnel started by suggesting that my grade book was evidence that I kept attendance in a manner against state regulation. He also brought up the vulnerability of my state teaching certification, preparing me for what I later learned was a common practice by administrators—offering to take my resignation in place of any further proceedings that "would hurt my career." These three people let me know that they were looking for anything they could use against me.

A few days later, I was told that the three of them had asked educators in the district to watch the drama tapes and write observations about what they saw. When the administrators didn't like what the educators wrote, each educator was asked to rewrite the observations—one person having to do so three times. At the trial, these educators testified that the implied messages were pretty clear: until they included negative comments about my project with my students, their write-ups would be sent back for "revision." These district decision makers had no regard for my twenty-five-year exemplary career, but the only way their abuse of power would be acceptable was if other people didn't know what their standard practices were. First they intimidated, and then they offered the alternative of resignation. When I chose a public forum to fight the charges against me, the media shone a light on the Ferguson-Florissant School District's administrators and school board, exposing the district to public view and public criticism as well as ridicule.

My supporters and I began the school board hearing knowing the odds we faced. The lawyer who represented the administrators and argued their case was also the lawyer for the school board. If a school board ignored the dismissal recommendation of their administrators and supported the teacher, they would undermine the leaders of their district, to say nothing of the lack of faith they would show in their own legal counsel. Still, we believed that, at their core, this school board wanted to focus on the students' best interests, the truth, the integrity of the classroom, and their community's commitment to public education. We believed that if abuses that had taken place were exposed, the school board would take action to remedy the situation.

My attorney began the hearing by saying,

"My name is Lisa Van Amburg, and I represent Dr. Cissy Lacks, a twenty-five-year veteran teacher of this district. We will prove to you tonight that these charges have absolutely no merit whatsoever. Rather, they are part of a reckless, deliberate, and malicious scheme by several administrators in this district to fire a master teacher, whose teaching methods have been proven to work . . . we will prove to you that the actions taken by Dr. John Wright and Mr. Vernon Mitchell, with the assistance of Ms. Barbara Davis, were taken in utter disregard, not only of this teacher's rights, but of the rights of her students to learn."

The district called the assistant superintendent of personnel as its witness. He said he couldn't interpret curriculum directives and that we'd have to ask the assistant superintendent of curriculum. The law firm, which represented both the administrators and the school district, showed the tapes of my students to the school board but they positioned the screen to face the audience of over four hundred, including numerous TV cameras from local stations. School board members had to move their chairs to see the screen. And they submitted Reginald's first poems.

My attorney wanted to show how the process of learning takes place in a classroom. We brought in respected educators, both from the district and the St. Louis community, to testify. Students involved in the writing of the drama exercises testified, as did my students from years past. Parents came forward and even other brave administrators from the district testified that they had never thought that the student discipline code could be used in the way it was being used in my case. I testified, using my time to illustrate the teaching techniques I had used successfully for twenty-five years.

In the termination hearing before the school board, the principal testified that I had been warned about allowing students to use profanity in the newspaper. I had started a newspaper and journalism class at the high school, and he said the first edition printed the F word and the S word, among others. He said that he had to call me in and tell me to never allow these words again and then he said he asked to preview every newspaper thereafter. The only true part was that he did ask to preview every newspaper. The rest was made up and neither the F word nor the S word was in the first newspaper.

His accusation was a matter of fact, not a "he said, she said" situation. When he testified, he said he didn't have the first edition with him. We brought it in the next day and submitted it as evidence. No such words were in the newspaper. He had made the whole thing up. Nevertheless, the school board findings cited testimony of the principal Vernon Mitchell as evidence that I had been warned previously about allowing my students to use profanity.

Perhaps we should have known better than even to try. The same legal counsel who represented the administrators wrote the findings that the school board president signed in my official dismissal. Later, one school board member, in deposition and under oath, testified that the school board had never discussed the student discipline code as it applied to my case and had discussed only one or two of the twenty-three findings listed in my dismissal. It was understood, without saying, that the others had been the creation of the lawyer to make a legal case for the district.

Another board member said in the deposition getting ready for trial, "And I'm the only one who made my vote public. I voted to terminate her." She repeated that expression so often during her deposition that when she said "terminate her," I heard it like a chant—*Terminate her... Terminate her... Terminate her... Terminator,* and I began to wonder if she was afraid of me because she thought I had the power of an Arnold Schwartzenegger character, which I could have assured her I did not. She did say she was sure I thought I had done nothing wrong and she was afraid that if I returned to the district, I would teach as I had taught before.

As it happened, getting fired brought me more than fifteen minutes of fame. Instead of lighting up like a sparkler and then fizzling out, my story grew, slowly and seriously, from the Midwest to the rest of the nation. *Education Week,* a newspaper for educators, published a story titled, "Expletive Deleted." The author said she did not choose the title because of the language in the student dramas but because she had come to realize in her investigation that these Ferguson-Florissant administrators and board members viewed me as the "expletive deleted."

Her article was reprinted for the cover story of *Teacher,* a national magazine, and even I had a hard time admitting it was me on the tabloid-sized, four-color, glossy cover, a picture of me with my hands reaching out as if I wanted to grab the readers and pull them into my story. The dramatic effect of that cover was, "This teacher has a story to tell." At least that's what the *Dateline NBC* producer said when he called to say *Dateline* was interested in doing a segment on me.

In our phone conversation, he said, "We're going to look at all sides, but this story is going to be about teaching." Others wanted to talk about profanity. *Dateline* wanted to talk about teaching. I did the story.

The highs and lows of my emotional life were almost always in the extreme. I can't remember having too many ordinary days. Before my suit against the district was heard in court, I received the prestigious PEN award given, by Paul Newman and the international literary organization PEN, to a person who had defended the First Amendment at some risk to herself or himself.

Actor Paul Newman introduced me at the ceremony and began, "The battle to safeguard freedom of speech has its casualties in this country, too. . . ." The stature of the award was increased by the reputation and stature of the man who presented it.

I took deep breaths while he was talking. Then I heard him say my name, and I was at the podium. I closed with words I hadn't planned—words that came from the events of the last few days—from being on television as ABC's Person of the Week, from being onstage at Lincoln Center, and from listening to Paul Newman talk about me.

> I understand the awesome responsibilities that go with this award. I understand my obligations to speak about teaching and about writing, and I welcome the opportunities that have been and will be given to me. I thank you for taking this public position in my support, and I want you to know that I will not let you or myself down.

I learned later how hard it was going to be to keep that pledge.

Before the jury trial, the Federal District Judge, Catherine Perry, ruled on Count One of my case, reversing the board's dismissal and ordering my reinstatement. Among other things, she wrote:

> The record as a whole clearly indicates that there was in practice an unwritten exception in the district for profanity in class-related activities. The evidence presented to the board was overwhelming that many administrators and teachers in the district allowed class-related profanity depending on the context and degree of profanity. . . . Defendant submitted no evidence indicating that the district in fact enforced policy 3043 to prohibit students from reading aloud or otherwise using profanity in creative works.

The district refused her reinstatement order. Only an injunction and a long appeal battle would get me back in the classroom, and then the trial would be postponed until this reinstatement order went through required appellate procedures. I would be in legal land forever. My attorney and I decided not to fight the district's refusal to obey the Judge Perry's reinstatement order. I didn't see that we had any choice. A teacher, I learned, had little clout outside of her classroom and now, I had to face, not too much clout inside, either.

In the courtroom, my attorney put the legal issues in lay terms before the jury:

> You're here to decide a case about a teacher of high school English in a troubled school where many kids are not interested in education, how she motivates the kids to write, how she turns them on to the value of poetry, how she gets them to engage in poetry contests, short story writing contests,

work on a high school newspaper, and sign up for journalism class. We're asking you to decide whether the district can summarily terminate a teacher who uses a time-honored teaching technique called the student-centered learning technique, which is the technique recommended by the Ferguson-Florissant School District, and we're also asking you to decide whether the illegal, racially motivated fears of two administrators, Vernon Mitchell and John Wright, were a consideration in the firing of Cissy Lacks.

The witnesses who had been at the school board hearing testified again, but at the jury trial another witness came forward; that witness was Reginald McNeary.

He told the jurors:

I was not going to try, and Ms. Lacks explained to us that writing was just what's inside of you, what you feel, and what's on your mind, and anybody could write that. I mean, it's really hard to write what somebody else wants you to write, because you have to have their standards, and you have, it's like they might not like it, ... but it was brought to us in a way we could understand it, and I picked up from that.

My attorney asked him if the first poems he wrote reflected anything inside of him at the time.

I guess hatred and anger. I really don't like to talk about those first poems. They are embarrassing.

He continued to tell the jury about how he became a poet.

It was like I woke up, or whatever, because I never knew that I had the potential or ability that I had, and so now, it was like easy ... write what you feel and what's on your mind, so I was writing, I was writing like, I would say, within a month, I had about eight poems, I was writing songs, and I started a book, a book ... when this month was over, it was like this is powerful.

He told the jurors what would have happened if I had censored those first poems.

I probably wouldn't have wrote again. I probably would have told her something. ... I mean, it's just like, to come out of, I don't think you understand where I was at, and I was not really participating, so to write anything, if I was just to write my name would be like a big or valiant effort, and if I was to come out of my shadow and write something and somebody was to criticize me, I would be mad. It would hurt my feelings, too. I probably wouldn't have came to the class again.

During the courtroom trial in a federal district court, we called Vernon Mitchell to testify regarding what he had told the board members, under oath, about profanities in the first newspaper:

My attorney, Lisa Van Amburg: When you testified under oath to the Board of Education in Ms. Lacks' termination matter, you told them that the first issue of the paper, the *Berkeley Bulldog Express* had profanity in it, did you tell them that?

Vernon Mitchell: Yes.

LV: You told them that under oath, didn't you?

VM: Yes.

LV: And you told them that you had talked to Cissy about profanity in the newspaper after the first issue came out, didn't you?

VM: Yes.

LV: You also told the board under oath, Mr. Mitchell, that the F word was in the first issue of the student newspaper, didn't you?

VM: Yes.

LV: What word were you referring to?

VM: *Fuck*, is that what you want me to say? That was the F word.

LV: You told the board the word *fuck* was in the first issue of the newspaper?

VM: Yes.

LV: You also told the board the word *shit* was in the first issue of the newspaper, didn't you?

VM: Yes.

LV: Mr. Mitchell, I'll show you what's been marked as Plaintiff's Exhibit 35, which is the *Berkeley Bulldog Express* newspaper, and the first issue is on the top of that stack there.

Would you take the first issue and tell us where the word *fuck* appears in the newspaper and where the word *shit* appears in the newspaper?

VM: I don't see it in there.

LV: So you told the board a lie, didn't you, Mr. Mitchell?

VM: One of the newspapers, and I thought it was the first issue, did have those words in it, and that's what I was responding to.

LV: Mr. Mitchell, you approved of all the other issues of the newspaper that came out after the first issue, isn't that true?

VM: No, it's not.

LV: After the first issue, sir, nothing got published without your approval, isn't that correct?

VM: No, the answer was no.

LV: Mr. Mitchell, do you recall me asking you at the board termination hearing in March of 1995 the following question on page 179? Question: "In fact, nothing gets published in those papers without your approval, isn't that true?" And your answer was, "After my conversation with, after the first paper, then it has to have my approval, that is correct." Was that true when you testified?

VM: Yes.

Although I was never able to talk to the jurors, I suspected they were indignant at the testimony of Vernon Mitchell. I knew that I was. But, at the time, I didn't know that the meaning of *indignant* hadn't come close to being defined.

Reginald and the other students who testified on my behalf made me so proud to be a teacher. Their bravery, earnestness, and articulateness under such pressure were more than admirable. At the same time, the principal, his supporting administrators, and board members made me ashamed to be part of that district and public education. Their distortions, their lies, and their lack of educational concerns were frightening indicators of how their decisions were made and enforced.

After three and a half years of waiting and preparing, two weeks of trial, and seven hours of jury deliberation, we had a verdict.

"On First Amendment claim, number one, did plaintiff have reasonable notice that allowing students to use profanity in their creative writing was prohibited?"

"No."

I looked at the jurors. Each one of them was looking directly at me. For the first time in the two years since I had been fired, my body relaxed.

"Number two, did defendant School District have a legitimate academic interest in prohibiting profanity by students in their creative writing, regardless of any other competing interest?"

"No."

Then the judge announced the verdict on the race discrimination claim.

"On the claim of plaintiff Cecilia Lacks against defendant Ferguson Reorganized School District R-2 for race discrimination, we find in favor of plaintiff Cecilia Lacks."

"Has it been proven by a preponderance of the evidence that defendant would have discharged plaintiff regardless of her race?"

"No."

I bent my head into my hands and then raised it to look at the jury again. I wanted to talk to them, to thank them, but the judge said to them:

I need to warn you about what may be obvious. You may be contacted by the news media and asked about this case . . . and you are free to handle any such requests any way you want . . . I wouldn't be surprised if you walk out of the building and there will be people there . . .

All the jurors left together, escorted by the guard. I thought I'd get to thank the jurors. I had wanted to so much. We opened the door to the courthouse entrance and below us was a row of camera lights shining up the courthouse stairs. It was dark and a little cold. The lights reflected off the night air, illuminating vapor clouds in front of us and blurring the reporters at the bottom of the stairs. For a second, I remembered the day I was fired and then I announced, "We won. Teachers and students won."

I believed then what my attorneys told me about the legal system: "Juries decide fact. Judges decide law." Along with that proposition, almost everyone in the legal field said that my case couldn't be overturned. The facts were too strong; the jury verdicts were too firm.

As we expected, the district appealed the decision. I could never have predicted what happened during oral argument in the eighth Circuit Court of Appeals, but I predicted what was going to happen afterwards.

I got concerned almost immediately when Richard Arnold, who was chief presiding judge of the eighth Circuit, asked my attorney why Mitchell's statement about being bothered by "black folks acting a fool and white folks videotaping it," was part of our race claim. At first, I thought he was joking, but I soon found out that he wasn't.

He began to ask questions as if the findings from the school board were true, even though we had disproved them at trial and I was told he had to take the facts of the jury trial in my favor as the true ones. When my attorney protested, Richard Arnold asked him if he was now telling school boards whom they were supposed to believe and not believe. It was as if the jury trial had never taken place.

Another judge inquired of my attorney, "A teacher as intelligent as Dr. Lacks, must it be assumed that she has to be led by the hand?"

Although the question didn't seem to have any relevance to appeal procedures and certainly had been covered during the trial, still, I was wishing for my attorney to defend me, to answer the question. *Tell him that I knew exactly what I was doing, that I'm a master teacher who has great success with her students and keeps up on the research for the teaching of language arts. Tell him that the jury heard the record and made the decision about whether I knew what I was doing or not.* But my appeal attorney, no longer the one I had at my jury trial, interpreted the question as rhetorical and did not respond. I wanted to interrupt the proceedings and defend myself. Although I knew that speaking out from the visitors' gallery would have shocked everyone, sometimes, now, I wish I had.

When my attorney tried to bring up the testimony of expert witnesses, Richard Arnold interrupted him and said not to talk to him about expert witnesses. A few weeks ago, in another case, one of them had said students should use rap to learn how to write and it would never happen as far as he was concerned.

I didn't understand at all what was taking place. I had been told these judges couldn't retry the case; they could only respond to legal issues arising from Judge Perry's rulings. Clearly, they had other things on their mind. I left the courtroom discouraged and disheartened. My attorney said I was overreacting. I knew that I wasn't. These men didn't have any idea of how to teach, how to reach students, what was going on in the real world of schools and yet they were ready to make judgments based upon their attitudes about learning and culture, not about their responsibilities to interpret law. I was in deep trouble; teachers were in deep trouble. These men were going to do great harm to students because they decided they knew so much more than all of us that they didn't have to listen to us or to the jury or pay any attention to the record.

Even though I knew the case was in trouble, their written opinion five months later was a sickening shock. They overturned every single jury verdict and Judge Perry's reinstatement. They began by saying:

> We reverse and remand for the entry of judgment in favor of the defendant school district. We hold, among other things, that a school district does not violate the First Amendment when it disciplines a teacher for allowing students to use profanity repetitiously and egregiously in their written work.

It was all about profanity and nothing else. Reinstatement was gone. Fair warning was gone. Legitimate academic purpose was gone. Title VII, race discrimination, was gone. I wondered where it all went. Where did they put it? For the sake of ruling on *profanity*, three judges dismissed the law.

Then they proceeded to overturn the factual decisions of the case regarding fair warning:

> After a careful review of the evidence, we hold that the record contains sufficient evidence for the school board to have concluded that Lacks willfully violated board policy.

In the opinion, Richard Arnold wrote:

> The court may not substitute its judgment of the evidence for that of the school board, and it must consider all evidence in the light most favorable to the decision of the board. The determination of the credibility of the witnesses is a function of the school board, not the reviewing court...

Lacks claimed that Mitchell never warned her about the use of profanity in the newspaper. However, under Missouri law, assessing the credibility of witnesses is the function of the school board, not the reviewing court. Because the school board heard testimony that Lacks was directly warned by the principal in her school that including "S blank blank T" and "F blank blank K" in the student newspaper violated the school board's profanity policy, the board could have reasonably found that Lacks knew that profanity was not allowed in students' creative activities.

They dismissed the First Amendment claim as easily:

We reverse and hold, as a matter of law, that the answer to both of those questions was "yes."

The race claim was the same:

We reverse and hold as a matter of law that race was not a motivating factor in the school board's decision to terminate Lacks. . . . The idea that the board "had race on its mind" when it fired Lacks . . . is questionable, especially given that the president of the school board, who signed the statement, testified that she did not believe that Lacks's case involved racial issues.

Now, school board members decided not only the credibility of the witnesses at the hearing, but they also decided the credibility of their own testimony at the trial.

As far as I could tell, Richard Arnold, who had written the opinion, did so as if the trial had never taken place, as if the jurors hadn't heard witness testimony, as if evidence hadn't been submitted to them. I remembered the fear I had when my first attorney, Lisa Van Amburg, told me that the administrators and their lawyer had thrown away Reginald's last three poems and submitted into evidence only the first two crude ones. That same sick panic returned.

I thought my school board hearing was the definition of "kangaroo court." I had no idea that an appellate judge would or could not only blatantly disregard evidence but also use false evidence to suit his position. His disregard for the basis of our legal system didn't seem to concern him, but I, and teachers across the country who were following my case, were as disillusioned as children who realized that the tooth fairy didn't exist. I didn't know how my belief in the legal system would ever be restored, and I wondered if Arnold had any concern over the damage he had done to me and to teachers and to our faith in the legal system so important for us to share with our students.

We did get his message, though. School board members could do whatever they wanted to teachers. Tenure meant nothing. School policy meant nothing, except in how it was interpreted at a particular moment. Good teaching meant nothing. Negotiated agreements were inconsequential.

We asked for the entire eighth Circuit to reconsider the case. They refused. One of the judges, Justice Theodore McMillian, wrote an opinion in dissent, requesting them to reconsider:

> The outcome of this appeal does not affect only the parties to this action. It affects all innovative and well-meaning teachers like Lacks and students in need like Reginald. When good educators are scared away or driven from our schools because they cannot trust the system to treat them honestly and fairly, we are all affected, most especially our children . . .
>
> In this day and age, while our children are being exposed to the worst aspects of society through the media, entertainment, and sometimes even in their own homes, we expect public school teachers to erase the effects of that environment and make even the most uninspired children learn and achieve. Meanwhile, we require our teachers to pick their way through a minefield of competing and conflicting expectations, and changing and elusive legal standards. This case stands for the proposition that, for all her hard work and devotion to all her students, this teacher was in the end fired for stepping on a political land mine—one which she never even knew was there. This case was wrongly decided . . .

We asked for my case to be heard before the Supreme Court. Fifteen national education organizations signed an amici brief on behalf of my case and on behalf of public education. In it, they said:

> [This] case presents the issue of whether it is constitutionally permissible to make a teacher a scapegoat or fire her for using a particular teaching technique that she had used for years, without first putting her on notice that use of that method is no longer permitted . . . the decision [of the eighth Circuit] promises to create serious confusion and even alarm and dismay among educators around the country, who must guard now what they say and teach. This Court should review the obviously flawed decision of the Eighth Circuit because it raises issues of great import to the governance of the public education system, and because of the need for greater uniformity and predictability in the implementation of important constitutional issues.

My case was not taken. The appeal decision was the final one.

Often, after I was fired, I was asked to speak to teachers beginning their careers. I said that I wished them the same joy, frustration, and pleasure in being with students that I experienced in my career. I wished them the same long-term relationships I had with many of my students. I wished them the opportunity to have dialogues with students that allow them to establish a sacred classroom space, one in which respect, trust, and joy permeated the learning activities. I wished them the opportunity to see their students become productive adults.

Also, I told them that for every lesson planned, for every assignment made, I didn't want any person to teach in fear of losing a job. I didn't want any classroom teacher or any class of students to fall prey to such a chilling effect on learning. I told them my message to my attorney: the legacy you create for me and for all teachers must be the right one. I didn't want my name to be associated with the case that struck fear in the hearts and minds of every teacher. And certainly, I didn't want self-censorship to take place because teachers were afraid. I wanted a strong statement to be made for academic freedom and teachers' rights to teach because those practices were critical for good education.

What I wanted did not happen. I am left with more unanswered than answered questions. How could I make sense of such craziness? Did some group of lawyers get together and concoct a horrible travesty of what teachers and school board members had negotiated in good faith over hours and years of conversation? But then why did board members go along with it? And how could judges say that a school board could believe whatever it wanted—with direct evidence to the contrary, with an opposing jury decision from two and a half weeks of testimony and with a federal district judge hearing everything and reinstating me? How could so many people in decision-making positions ignore educational research, disregard civil rights issues, distort material and evidence, and lie under oath? And pretty much get away with all of it.

The lesson I learned is one I regret having to share. I have come to realize that these people didn't know, didn't care to know, and didn't care to learn what goes on in a classroom and why. And in many ways it's not useful to speculate about motive because the point is what happened to me could happen in any school district. The conditions seem to be ripe for this kind of abuse of civil rights. The aftermath is the fear that teachers have and the harm those fears create in students' education.

I am still trying to make sense of the experience and how telling the story might help students and teachers. I remember and still plan to keep the pledge I made at the PEN ceremony, that *I understand my obligations to speak about teaching and about writing, and I welcome the opportunities that have been and will be given to me.* I keep with me Justice McMillian's thoughts: *When good educators are scared away or driven from our schools because they cannot trust the system to treat them honestly and fairly, we are all affected, most especially our children.*

This attack on teachers and on education needs to draw the attention an epidemic requires. Teachers afraid to teach produce students afraid to learn and a society in turmoil because its citizens are afraid and unable to deal honestly and effectively with the realities confronting them.

Cissy Lacks continues to live in St. Louis, where she works as a medical writer and freelance photographer. She exhibits her photography in one-woman shows, pursues her creative writing projects, and continues her commitment to speak on educational issues. She can be reached by email at cissylacks@earthlink.net. Further information can be obtained on the Web at <http://www.home.earthlink.net/~cissylacks>.

11

Portraits of Courage
Test Defiers and the Fruits of Resistance

GLORIA PIPKIN AND
RELEAH COSSETT LENT

Hope isn't a choice, it's a moral obligation, a human obligation, an obligation to the cells in your body.... Hope is not naive, hope grapples endlessly with despair. Real, vivid, powerful, thunderclap hope, like the soul, is at home in darkness, is divided; but lose your hope and you lose your soul.... Will the world end if you act? Who can say? Will you lose your soul... if you don't act, if you don't organize? I guarantee it.

—Tony Kushner, May 26, 2002
Commencement speech at Vassar College

*A*merican schools are under siege. Emphasizing the bottom line, data-driven decision making, and children as products, politicians and bureaucrats have imposed on our schools a misguided business model based on standards that work for auto parts but not for nonstandard children. In every state but Iowa, the standardization of education has been accompanied by high-stakes tests used to determine promotion, graduation, school ranking and funding, and bonuses for teachers and administrators. Scores on a single, flawed test are used to make life-altering decisions for our children.

Because test scores reign supreme, the quest for higher numbers cannibalizes the curriculum, diverts scarce resources, stigmatizes poor test-takers, sends push-out rates soaring, and turns our schools into test prep centers. Real books are replaced by practice tests and workbooks, and writing in a variety of modes, forms, and genres for a range of authentic purposes fades into formulaic writing-in-a-box that penalizes creativity and produces prose no one would ever choose to write or read.

This bleak picture will only worsen as the federal government imposes new testing requirements and policing measures under the so-called "No Child Left Behind" Act (more accurately dubbed the "No Child Left Untested" Act by pundits). Not only will more tests be required in many states, but teaching methods and materials will also be prescribed and reviewed by a panel of seventy-three experts—only one of whom is a teacher. The new buzzwords are "scientifically based reading instruction" and "direct, intensive, systematic, extensive, comprehensive" training in reading methods approved by the federal government. Last fall we were given a bone-chilling look at reading under the new regime, when George W. Bush visited a Sarasota, Florida, school and beamed approvingly as children read a dull, monosyllabic story in unison to a metronomic beat clapped out by their teacher, and responded on cue to her hand signals. Welcome to Stepford Schools.

But as the voices of Steve Orel, James Hope, and Teresa Glenn have already demonstrated, in dark times the stars begin to shine. In this chapter we feature other heroines and heroes among the Resistance to high-stakes testing. Most are teachers whose opposition has led them to take costly stands against harmful testing. One lost his job; others have been suspended and threatened with revocation of teaching licenses. We are also honored to include the stories of a parent and community activist who took on another divisive and destructive form of ranking and sorting—school tracking—in Selma, Alabama, and of a high school valedictorian who used her commencement speech as an occasion to oppose the testing obsession.

The spirit of these courageous people is summed up by Bruce Degi of Colorado, who wrote, "Perhaps I just taught Gandhi and Thoreau and M.L.K., Jr. for too long. I guess I actually started believing that when something is wrong, seriously wrong, that you don't compromise, you don't quibble, you just say no."

Mitch Balonek: Sick of Testing

When English teacher Mitch Balonek prohibited his fourteen-year-old daughter from taking the state-required proficiency test in October of 2000, one that must be passed for students to graduate, other teachers in his school agreed with him philosophically, but were reluctant to take such a public stand against high-stakes testing. What must they have thought when, a few months later, he refused to give the test to ninth graders at Scott High, an inner-city school attended predominantly by minorities in Toledo, Ohio? His answer is that he was using his sick leave to stay home during the scheduled testing time as a way of showing teachers how they can protest and not get fired. Besides, he says, if he had been there "I'm afraid I might have been tempted to help them."

He is adamant in defense of his students, many of whom already lead stressful lives not only at school, but at home as well. "We cheat these kids out of diplomas that they worked very hard for, particularly in the inner city where 50 to 60 percent of the kids drop out." He points out that the cultural bias is immediately apparent when considering how many of the students have kids of their own or must work more hours than they attend school for economic reasons. "Proficiency tests," he says succinctly, "cannot measure human potential."

While some may have viewed Balonek as radical, he saw his actions as a type of civil disobedience that he hoped would propel the antitesting movement forward. The following year, however, he took a different approach. While still expressing disdain for the testing system to anyone who would listen, he agreed to administer the tests and tutor students who had not passed. His concern was that if the students failed the test, they would feel discounted as well as denied a diploma, a necessity for higher education and better jobs. Interestingly, Balonek's daughter, a tenth grader now, still refuses to take the five Ohio Ninth Grade Proficiency Tests. Although it has been difficult for her socially, she, like her father, says she is proud to be a leader in the high-stakes testing opposition—and determined to be successful without the official state stamp identifying her as "Proficient."

Bill Cala: A Superintendent's "Constructive Rebellion" Against Testing

Like school officials all over the country, Dr. William C. Cala, superintendent of the Fairport Central Schools in upstate New York, has seen firsthand the negative effects of high-stakes testing on the school system he oversees: increased dropout rates, widening gap between performance of white students and minorities, impossible hurdles for students with disabilities, and sacrifice of rich curricula to demands of test preparation. Unlike most school officials, who generally support the party line, Bill Cala has become an outspoken critic of the New York State Regents exams.

Despite a repressive political climate that rewards yes-men, Cala has written and spoken widely in professional publications and at conferences, seminars, classes, and community forums about the harms of high-stakes testing. In June of 2001 he took the campaign to the New York State Assembly, where he told legislators that he was "saddened, shocked, and disillusioned" by the disproportionate harms the one-size-fits-all testing scheme inflicts on disadvantaged students and those in vocational programs.

Joining with parents, teachers, principals, university researchers, and community activists in the Rochester/Buffalo area, Cala helped organize a grassroots group called Coalition for Common Sense in Education to "raise questions, encourage critical debate and strategic action in response to the burgeoning use of high-stakes standardized tests in our schools." A major focus of CCSE efforts has been to organize citizens to bring pressure to bear on the New York State Assembly. Cala and other CCSE members were among hundreds who marched on the Capitol in Albany in May of 2001 to protest the tyranny of testing.

Bill Cala's activism has not been restricted to protests, however. In what Alfie Kohn has called "an intriguing and constructive form of rebellion" against the Regents exams, Cala joined a group of superintendents from the Rochester area to create an independent local school board with the authority to award an alternative diploma based on multiple forms of assessment. Writing in *The School Administrator* (December 2001), Cala said that "To accept the collateral damage of additional dropouts in the name of higher education is unacceptable."

A board of directors comprising representatives from business and industry as well as all levels of education will establish criteria for the alternate diploma, govern the process of setting it up, and serve as grantors of the diploma, which will also be accompanied by a certificate of employability. Cala hopes to have the new program that will include three avenues leading to a diploma in place by 2003.

Bill Cala can be reached at Wcala@Rochester.rr.com. *Contact the Coalition for Common Sense in Education at P.O. Box 10606, Rochester, NY 14610 (585) 234-0189.*

Bruce Degi: Just Saying No to High-Stakes Testing

BRUCE DEGI, AN ENGLISH TEACHER AT CHERRY CREEK HIGH SCHOOL IN Denver, resigned early in 2001 rather than give the Colorado Student Assessment Program (CSAP) tests. In his fourth year of teaching after twenty-two years in the Air Force, Degi retired as a lieutenant colonel. As a Senior Fulbright Scholar, he taught at the University of Veszprem in Hungary as well as at the Air Force Academy, where he was a tenured associate professor of English. Before moving to Cherry Creek High School, Degi taught Advanced

Placement (AP) and International Baccalaureate (IB) courses as well as other English courses at another high school in the same district.

In a *Denver Post* article, staff writer Susan Wallace notes that Degi views CSAP as based on a business model of education that represents "identification and punishment" rather than education reform. We asked Degi to elaborate on these themes.

––––––––––––––––––––––––––––––––––––

One (and only one) of the major problems I have with CSAP is the "school report card" aspect that follows on the heels of the testing. I am afraid that we are still in the grips of the American Puritan spirit. Much like what happens in *The Scarlet Letter,* I see one of the major functions of this exam as identifying the "bad" people among us (in this case, schools) thus forcing those bad people to be the object of public scorn and humiliation. In Colorado, in direct defiance of one of the main principles of "standards-based education," a percentage of schools will be (must be) identified as "non-adequate." And why is that identification so important to our modern-day (Republican) Puritans? For the same reason: We can feel so much better about ourselves when we see others in the community forced to wear the scarlet letter. If they are "bad," we must be "good." This was the major problem I had in deciding to leave or remain with my school.

The district's policy toward the CSAP was "we're going to do as well as possible on this exam—be the best in the state—and then we can use that position of strength to force changes and compromise with the state in the future." (An attitude I find sadly naive.) Like all districts, the students were then bribed to attend school during the testing period (drawings for prizes, etc.). I could not be a part of that. I saw myself as part of public education in Colorado, not just as a part of the [Cherry] Creek District. I find it unacceptable to celebrate a "victory" (if that is what it is) that causes needless pain and suffering to my colleagues in other districts.

Calling standardized tests "the culmination of an insidious change in paradigm over the past decades in America concerning our schools," Degi goes on to say that "Schools are now just another business; teachers are simply assembly-line workers who produce a product that we have to 'quality control' during the manufacturing process. The business metaphor subverts and perverts everything I believe about education, every reason why I became a teacher."

Degi says that the roots of his resistance go way back. "Perhaps I just taught Gandhi and Thoreau and M.L.K., Jr. for too long. I guess I actually started believing that when something is wrong, seriously wrong, that you don't compromise, you don't quibble, you just say no."

Since his resignation Degi is teaching as an adjunct at Metropolitan State College in Denver and learning real-time transcription for deaf college students.

Cathy Kitto and Mary Compton: Refusing the State's Bribe Money

One of the most pernicious aspects of Florida's school grading plan is that it diverts scarce funds from the neediest schools and gives bonuses to those with higher scores on the Florida Comprehensive Assessment Test (FCAT). At Gulf Gate Elementary School in Sarasota, principal Cathy Kitto and four teachers decided they couldn't in good conscience accept their share of the state's bribe money. The five educators took a day of personal leave in December of 1999 to fly to Tallahassee and present a check for $2,540—the amount of their combined bonuses—to Governor Jeb Bush and the state board of education at a hearing on the controversial school grading plan.

Gulf Gate teacher Mary Compton told the Florida board of education that the pressures of the state's high-stakes test had led schools to sacrifice rich learning experiences for canned programs that promise their schools "won't end up on the wrong side of the bell curve." Compton held up a copy of *Johnny Tremaine,* an award-winning children's book about the American Revolution that "burns forever in the hearts of my students," and told the board that books like this were being replaced by test prep workbooks. Warning of the dangers that a rigid state-mandated testing program poses to intellectual freedom, Compton said, "Fear is doing away with any original thoughts in our schools."

Following Compton on the agenda, Cathy Kitto gave another example of how testing pressures eviscerate the curriculum. At the end of the school's annual arts day, which brought visual and performing artists from the community onto the campus and gave children an opportunity to experience and participate in a variety of art forms, a teacher remarked, "Well, another day shot not practicing for the FCAT." Other teachers wanted to close the school's state-of-the-art science lab for the entire month of January in order to do more test prep.

Kitto also spoke to the demoralizing effects of labeling schools on the basis of test scores. "We don't believe that we worked harder or better than our sister schools in Sarasota, or throughout Florida, who received lesser grades. We think every school has a difficult job to do. I don't know . . . of one school that's slacking in its effort. Every school needs more funding, every teacher needs to be compensated better. And that's why we are returning the bonuses that we received for being an A school."

Jeb Bush responded with contempt to the Sarasota teachers' pilgrimage and symbolic gesture. "Five or six teachers are making a big grandstand play," he said before the Cabinet meeting. "It really won't change anything about this."

After the Sarasota contingent returned home, the school superintendent admonished Cathy Kitto, telling her that her actions and comments as a principal reflected badly on the district. Since that time, Cathy Kitto has contributed her bonuses to state and national organizations that oppose high-stakes testing.

Stacey Miller: Giving Parents Choices

Legally, California teachers may inform parents of their right to opt their children out of standardized testing, but they are not allowed to "advocate" opting out. So, what happens if a teacher informs the parents of her non-English speaking students that they have a right to keep their children from taking a test given only in English? She gets reprimanded, placed on administrative leave, and threatened with revocation of her teaching certificate.

Stacey Miller, a nontenured teacher at J.W. Fair Middle School in the heart of Silicon Valley, found out the hard way in the spring of 2002 what can happen to teachers who dare inform parents of their legal rights to exempt their own children from taking the Standardized Testing and Reporting (STAR) exams. Several of the parents filed exemptions, but the principal talked them into withdrawing their requests. When Miller reassured them that the principal did not have the authority to deny their requests, several parents resubmitted their waivers, but Miller was forced to give the students the tests anyway. Her local union provided her with an attorney, but it didn't stop the superintendent from accusing her of "disrupting my campus" at a school board meeting and angrily "sending her home" for the rest of the school term.

Why does it matter so much to school officials if parents exercise their rights by not allowing their children to take the much-debated high-stakes test? Perhaps the answer lies in President Bush's "No Child Left Behind" Act that ties accountability programs to federal Title I funding. California schools could lose funding if too many students opt out of taking the test, so more and more often teachers are faced with overt or implied gag orders so that the number of families who exercise the exemption does not increase. In addition, if more than 10 percent of a school's student population does not take the test, that school cannot qualify for bonuses in the state's Academic Performance Index.

Miller refuses to back down, however, despite pressure from her school district, citing the investigation as a First Amendment issue. The superintendent continues to insist that she crossed the line by "soliciting parents and students" to sign the requests for exemption. The investigation is ongoing, and although Miller was put on paid administrative leave, the message is a strong one to any teacher who might even be tempted to bring up the subject of standardized test waivers.

"As a teacher, it's my job to communicate with parents, and that's what I've always done," Miller told the San Jose *Mercury News*. The ACLU of California is considering Miller's case.

Rose Sanders: Fighting Educational Apartheid

Rose Sanders, an attorney and community activist in Selma, Alabama, took on the Selma Public Schools in 1990 and ended up in jail. Her daughter Ainka, nine years old at the time, was tracked into a low-level class despite her high academic achievements in previous grades. After Sanders confronted the teacher, Ainka was moved to a gifted class, but Sanders insisted that all of her classmates be moved from classes labeled "low level," ones she was convinced destroyed their self-esteem and opportunities for future success. The principal refused, forcing Sanders to appeal to the Selma School Board. Even as she argued for an end to "a system of American-style apartheid," nonwhite students in Selma schools remained victims of racist tracking and testing policies. Faced with near indifference by the board, Sanders and other parents boycotted the businesses of school board members, and students conducted a one-day boycott of the schools.

Still, the requests of the parents and students were ignored. In desperation, the parents paid a visit to the mayor. After being put off by his secretary and convinced that they would not be granted a meeting, Sanders tried to enter his office, knocking loudly on the door. She was denied entrance. Unaware that the police had been summoned and were not only outside on the grounds but throughout the building, Sanders placed her hand on the doorknob. Unexpectedly, a policeman came from behind and grabbed her around the neck. She was eventually dragged away by the police, along with two other people, and later hospitalized for cuts and bruises. That night, more than two thousand people jammed into a school board meeting, and a few days later, 150 students staged a sit-in at Selma High School. In response, the school board shut down the schools for five days and agreed to terminate the superintendent's job at the end of the year.

Even today, Sanders points out, most of the students and teachers accept the racially unequal tracking and testing policies without question. The students who suffer under this system are, according to Sanders, "part of the miseducated masses of people of color academically prepared and destined by design to be servants, fast-food workers, unskilled factory workers, welfare recipients, dropouts, never-employed persons, and prison inmates. Many leave school out of boredom while their 'superior peers' receive an education which is not in fact superior, but what any child in a democratic, technically advanced nation should receive."

Sanders continues to speak out against what she terms "the new segregation" and other educational injustices not only in Alabama, but all over the nation.

Annelise Schantz: Speaking Truth to Power

ANNELISE SCHANTZ DELIVERED THIS VALEDICTORY ADDRESS AT A HUDSON, Massachusetts, high school graduation in June of 2000. Governor Cellucci, a supporter of high-stakes tests, was on the stage at the time as Annelise received a standing ovation led by her fellow graduates.

Umm yeah, so I'm the valedictorian. Number one. But, what separates me from number 2, 3, 4, 5, 6, 50, or 120? Nothing but meaningless numbers. What really is the difference between 3.8, 2.9, and 1.5? All these randomly assigned numbers reflect nothing about the true character of an individual. They say nothing about personality. Nothing about desire or will. Nothing about values or morals. Nothing about intelligence. Nothing about creativity. Nothing about heart. Numbers cannot and will not ever be able to tell you who a person really is. Yet in today's society we are sadly becoming more and more number oriented. Schools today are being forced to teach to the numbers. Children are no longer learning because it is interesting and fun; they are learning to pass the test so that the school will continue to be funded. New mandates across the country and in our own state incorrectly correlate test scores with the worth of teachers and schools. Not once do these new mandates take into account that schools in low-income areas will never have as many books, long-term students, parent volunteers, or state-of-the-art facilities. How can anyone call these tests fair? Just as class rank and SAT scores say nothing about the true worth of a person, a child's or school's score on a test says nothing about the worth of the school or teachers.

It is disturbing enough that throughout high school, GPA and grades are pushed as the most important things, while learning, the real reason we are in school, falls by the wayside. The MCAS [Massachusetts Comprehensive Assessment System] serve as just another set of meaningless numbers that add one more reason to focus on scores and forget learning.

The already teetering learning process, made difficult by the social dynamics of school cliques, disrupted by a constant lack of funding and misplaced values, has been further torn apart by a few meddling politicians and yuppies who were bored and felt the need to create what they call a standard. Who cares that it is completely biased against those with learning disabilities and those in ESL programs. Who cares that the test itself is frighteningly ethnocentric in its rigid definition of what we should be learning. Who cares that all these numbers and standards only help to stamp out independent thought. All that matters is that the head honchos want some numbers that they can spew to the public to prove that they are so helpful to today's schoolchildren. Numbers, useless meaningless numbers. I doubt that a single one of these politicians has ever stopped to consider that we are not numbers. We are individuals. How dare they restrict us once more into useless categories of failing, proficient, advanced. Judging us by our competency on a biased test is perhaps the biggest injustice that the state could ever inflict upon us.

Useless information about the double helix shape of DNA or the square root of negative one will not help anyone to survive. Last time I checked, the properties of diffusion and osmosis were interesting but they still were of no help in reality. The battle of 1812 cannot help you prepare a healthy meal and common error C cannot help a jurist in a murder trial. Instead of realizing this, the bureaucracy that claims to be for the people continues to push for the advancement of uniform mediocrity in schools. Learning rote information never taught anyone to think. History, science, math, and English won't do you any good if you can't apply them. Formulaic thinking might help one to get good scores on tests but it doesn't do jack in reality.

When will society realize that the only useful skill that high school could ever teach us is the art of using our brain to think independently and express our ideas coherently? With the use of one's brain anything is possible, any problem solvable, any question answerable, any goal reachable. Unfortunately, it is the one thing that many students never learn because they are too busy trying to pass the tests.

Schools are being turned into factories churning out brainless, mindless, opinionless hacks year after year. Any student that challenges the system is labeled a difficulty. Any teacher that pushes the limits and forces their students to actually use their brains is chastised and labeled extreme. In my five years, I have seen too many wonderful teachers lost or restricted to the box. I have seen too many extraordinary kids give up on school. But no one cares.

The idea of MCAS is similar to putting a Band-Aid on a severed limb. Not only is it pointless, it is a waste of time that could be much better spent. The solution to the poor education of children is not a uniform curriculum and it is certainly not a test. The solution lies in equal and adequate funding for all schools. So that teachers are paid what they are actually worth and budgets don't have to choose between paper for the copy machine or books for the students. Perhaps it is the grand old elected officials' education that needs to be questioned. Public officials that can unflinchingly spend a third of the national budget on an unnecessary army and billions on the Big Dig to please commuters, but cannot hack up enough money to adequately fund schools and social service programs.

How are we supposed to grow up to be thinking individuals when the examples set for us are those of greedy politicians bought out by money in a corrupt democratic system where only the rich are allowed to participate? A corporate world where our parents whore themselves out to heartless companies that are only out to make a buck. A clothing and manufacturing industry that moves to the third world so that it can freely underpay and abuse its workers in order to make the most profit. A world where our education is reduced down to GPA, SAT, and MCAS. Maybe our society should worry less about the three R's and more about the morals of future generations, and leave the teaching to the teachers.

There are some who have managed to grow beyond the memorized facts and formulaic thinking. Those who were in Seattle at the WTO conference. Those that are in Harvard Square today protesting The Gap's labor and environmental policies. Those that will be protesting at this year's Republican and Democratic national conventions. Those that are trying to make a difference. But they are a miraculous few. They could be and should be so many more. We do community service and plant a few flowers but are never given the chance to truly understand what a community is. We participate in a student government but never learn what it truly means to be an activist. We are taught history but are never truly taught about the history that we have the chance to make.

We hear GPA, class rank, SAT, test grade, midterms, finals, scholastic achievement, but never once do we hear "never mind the grades, think about the learning, think about activism, think about life." We celebrate those who have earned good grades but don't bother to consider if they are at all worthy of the praise. Does anyone care about the human beings behind the numbers?

Perhaps I am bitter, but I have every right to be bitter and angry about the world that I see around me. My responsibility lies in that I must do something constructive with my anger. And I suppose that in the end I have school to thank for making me so unhappy, inadvertently giving me the fuel to take a stand in life and do something with what I have been given. And so I stand here today and forever, and refuse to be defined as a number.

George Schmidt: Exposing Tests to Public Scrutiny

For more than a quarter of a century, George Schmidt enjoyed a dual relationship with Chicago's public schools. He taught English at a number of inner-city schools, including Bowen High, and in recent years took on part-time duties as security coordinator for the school. After school hours, like an educationally focused Clark Kent, he wore another hat—as a critic of the system that employed him, working as a reporter and later as editor of *Substance*, a monthly newspaper founded in 1974 by a group of substitute teachers (which included Schmidt) to aid their struggle for better pay and working conditions.

When pilot forms of the citywide Chicago Academic Standards Examinations (CASE) were delivered anonymously to *Substance* early in 1999, George did what he expected his students to do—check for errors, even his own in grading their papers. What he found in CASE were flawed instruments riddled with sloppy editing, factual errors, and items with more than one correct answer.

On the world studies test, for example, students were asked which of the following items is determined by economic systems:

A. what trade should take place
B. what food and language
C. how much goods are worth
D. which people should be employed in certain jobs

Determined to expose the flaws of the test and open up public debate about their uses, George published sections of CASE, including the world studies test, in *Substance*'s January 1999 issue. After revealing the official correct answer as "C," George pointed out what would have been obvious to his students: "Imagine an economic system that didn't help determine trade or the kinds of employment people can have."

A few days later the Chicago School Reform Board of Trustees suspended George without pay and sued him and *Substance* for $1 million. Despite the fact that the tests he deemed a "curricular atrocity" had not been copyrighted until after George published them, the civil action cited him for copyright infringements and violation of trade secrets.

The school system's unprecedented action unleashed a barrage of publicity throughout the city. One television station showed an irate Mayor Richard M. Daley asking, "Who are these teachers? What kind of people are they? We should find out where they live."

In its motion for a temporary restraining order and a writ of seizure against George and *Substance*, the school board wrote, "The Newspaper and other materials already disseminated must be confiscated, even if it takes the U.S. Marshals going to every Chicago Public School teacher's home."

On April 2, 1999, George counter-sued the Chicago public schools for violation of his First Amendment rights.

On August 23, 2000, the Chicago school board fired George Schmidt, disregarding the written statement by the Illinois state hearing officer that Chicago needs more teachers like him.

Despite ongoing assaults on his professionalism and the loss of his livelihood, George has continued to speak out, in *Substance* and elsewhere, against testing abuses and the spurious claims advanced in their behalf by politicians, corporate executives, and bureaucrats. His trial date, originally set for September 2001, has been postponed several times. As of this writing, George Schmidt's professional and personal fate still hangs in the balance.

Subscribe to Substance *or contact Schmidt at 5132 West Berteau, Chicago, IL 60641.*

Afterword

Cowardice asks the question, Is it safe? Expediency asks the question, Is it politic? Vanity asks the question, Is it popular? But conscience asks the question, Is it right? And there comes a time when one must take a position that is neither safe, nor politic, nor popular, but he must take it because his conscience tells him that it is right.

— Dr. Martin Luther King, Jr.

Emily Dickinson wrote "I dwell in possibility" and it is in that place that the voices in this collection also dwell. This one factor sets them apart as models of courage, allowing their vision of what is possible to effect what seems impossible in America's schools. Even as Dickinson sat alone contemplating life's mysteries, each of these educators was forced to inhabit his or her own private place, a place of emotional pain and insecurity. The magnitude and importance of their individual struggles are only now becoming apparent, but like most great displays of courage, their acts will have far-reaching consequences for the majority who depend on the few to right the wrongs in society.

What qualities cause some to refuse to sign the proclamation, to wear the scarlet letter on behalf of those who speak but are not heard? Even an in-depth psychological study may not answer such a complex question. Within their individual stories differences begin to emerge, and the bright threads of integrity flash through the fabric. That sparkling trait creates the willingness to stand in the circle of fire and to risk losing credibility and career, as well as financial and emotional security. It is this passion for understanding their

141

own truths and an unwavering commitment to protect the rights of students that form the elements of their collective personalities.

Yet why is it that the rich tapestry they create does not fit into the entire educational picture? Is it that others in education do not feel the inner mandates that seem to propel these voices from the safety of the "norm" into a position of defending principles that protect the educational rights of all Americans? While many who have spoken out have enjoyed the support of like-minded thinkers, others have stood alone, pariahs even to those who acknowledge their truth. It is frightening to consider that those with the courage to defend the ideals that make education more than a bureaucratic progress report are the few voices opposing the decay that is infusing education.

The philosophical and psychological musings about these untraditional educators make for an interesting study, but meanwhile will the courageous voices resounding in these pages be loud enough to stem the cruel tide of high-stakes testing that reduces individual learners to same-size beans that are counted and sorted? Will policymakers continue to deny the inhumanity of pushing out hundreds of students in a major American city so that the system does not reflect the immensity of their needs? Will administrators and lawmakers continue to accuse and intimidate exemplary and dedicated teachers because they dare to question the use of flawed tests? Will the time come when teachers will not be viewed as subversives who empower students to take pride in their own cultures or encourage democratic processes that create thinking adults? Will a majority of educators eventually give in to the Orwellian urge to slip past Big Brother and answer the call of their consciences?

Many otherwise good-hearted, caring teachers and parents accept conditions they suspect are not best for students, indeed not best for anyone. It is as Shelley Fite, a student we taught many years ago, recounted: "The way I see it, every time a principal chases out a great teacher who challenges the system, he/she is just radicalizing a new crop of students. Teachers teach by example. If a teacher quietly accepts a system that is stifling her students, students learn to 'get by,' and to accept defeat. They learn that no one is willing to fight for them. If a teacher fights back—even if she loses or is forced to stop teaching—students learn to question ideas and challenge injustice, and they learn that education is worth fighting for."

The educators in this book have fought back, and in some cases have lost, but their dream is still vivid and possible: a fair, equal, and meaningful education for all of our children.

Recommended Reading

Bomer, Randy, and Katherine Bomer. 2002. *For a Better World: Reading and Writing for Social Action.* Portsmouth, NH: Heinemann.

Daly, James K., P. Schall, and R. Skeele, eds. 2001. *Protecting the Right to Teach and Learn: Power, Politics, and Public Schools.* New York: Teachers College Press.

Edelsky, Carole, ed. 1999. *Making Justice Our Project: Teachers Working Toward Critical Whole Language Practice.* Champaign-Urbana, IL: National Council of Teachers of English.

Garan, Elaine. 2002. *Resisting Reading Mandates: How to Triumph with the Truth.* Portsmouth, NH: Heinemann.

Kohn, Alfie. 2000. *The Case Against Standardized Testing: Raising the Scores, Ruining the Schools.* Portsmouth, NH: Heinemann.

Martinez, Elizabeth C., ed. 1991. *Five Hundred Years of Chicano History in Pictures: 500 Anos del Pueblo Chicano.* Albuquerque: Southwest Community Resources.

Ohanian, Susan. 1999. *One Size Fits Few: The Folly of Educational Standards.* Portsmouth, NH: Heinemann.

———. 2001. *Caught in the Middle: Nonstandard Kids and a Killing Curriculum.* Portsmouth, NH: Heinemann.

————. 2002. *What Happened to Recess and Why Are Our Children Struggling in Kindergarten?* New York: McGraw-Hill.

Palmer, Parker. 1998. *The Courage to Teach: Exploring the Inner Landscape of a Teacher's Life.* San Francisco: Jossey-Bass.

Pipkin, Gloria, and ReLeah Cossett Lent. 2002. *At the Schoolhouse Gate: Lessons in Intellectual Freedom.* Portsmouth, NH: Heinemann.

Shannon, Patrick. 1992. *Becoming Political: Readings and Writings in the Politics of Literacy Education.* Portsmouth, NH: Heinemann.

Shor, Ira, ed. 1999. *Education Is Politics: Critical Teaching Across Differences, K–12: A Tribute to the Life and Work of Paulo Freire.* Portsmouth, NH: Heinemann.

Temes, Peter S. 2002. *Against School Reform (And in Praise of Great Teaching).* Chicago: Ivan R. Dees.